To Robin an... (handwritten)

Harvey Dahline (handwritten signature)

Can Murder
Be Justified?

218-256-6666 (handwritten)

Written by
Harvey Dahline

Edited by
Doris Dahline
Steve Koskovich
Britta Arendt

Consultant
Ron Stoesz, brother

Copyright © 2017 Harvey Dahline

Acknowledgements:

Characters and names included in the stories within this book
are fictional, although some may be based on actual people and
experiences of the author.

Previous works by Harvey Dahline:

Dedication to Duty, published 2017

Cover design by Britta Arendt
Cover photo Beth Dahline

ISBN 978-0-692-98090-3

First edition
Printed in the United States of America

This book is dedicated to
Sgt. Alan Lee Dahline

MY SON

How does a father speak of a son that goes before him?

Memories come flooding back of a time so many years ago. His mother and I bringing Alan home to that cold little tar paper shack in the country. His crib next to our bed - we were so proud and happy!

Alan was always a happy child, forever amazing us, walking early. His first words were in sentences - "see the lights." In a short time, he knew all of his colors. Now I know he got this from his mother who I know is waiting for him.

Alan loved reading. He was not into sports as his brothers but more about taking care of his little sister Beth.

The years were flying by and he graduated. Then, he was into college and, in a short time, he joined the United States Air Force - going up the ranks.

After his service time of working in the medical field, he went to his one true love - the children's hospital in Denver, Colorado. Working for 37 years, he retired on June 1, 2017.

While going through his things, I found many letters of commendations for his work through the years of which he never mentioned to us. I also found an American flag which had been presented to Alan for his work which was flown over the United States Capitol for a day on Dec. 4, 1997. The reading stated: "This is to certify that this accompanying flag was flown over the United States Capitol on Dec. 4, 1997, at the request of the Honorable Michael N. Castle, Member of Congress."

This was our son.

CHAPTERS

PREFACE

I have written a book of nonfiction, "Dedication to Duty," and am wondering if I could write a book of fiction. All short stories: "Can Murder Be Justified?"

Having been a police officer for over 40 years, along the way you become concerned with the path our justice system is taking us. Where the Bible says, "an eye for an eye and a tooth for a tooth," our justice system seems to walk around this.

In this book, be it love or murder, I looked for diversity. You'll find each story is completely different from the others. The only exception being, they all come to a justifiable ending.

- Harvey Dahline

1
THE NECKLACE

The lady seemed to be in trouble. As Tex was driving up he could see her car, a BMW, setting just off the road. The deer lying in the ditch, a large buck. The front window caved in with damage to the front end.

This looked to be one of the opportunities he was always looking for. If he could pull this off, his scoreboard would be four.

Be soft, be gentle, don't scare her off. Late twenties, you might say well stacked and sure of herself as she stepped out onto the road to wave him down.

The others had been nice, not lasting too long after we'd gotten tired of them. This could be the prize of them all. Pulling slowly to the side of 169, it was still 20 miles from the town of Aitkin. Traffic had been light. Pulling up, rolling down the passenger side window, the lady approached. Trying not to be overly interested, he said, "Lady, do you need help, I could find a wrecker and send it back"? She was shivering; her breath could be seen in the cold air. Then, he added, "My name is Tex Landow."

At that she hesitated a moment, then she was saying, You're the first car by in half an hour, could I get in and warm up, should know better than to head out on a trip without a good coat, gloves and my phone." Looking at her he knew she was going to be something special. Acting concerned, asking if she had been hurt or if she wanted a ride to the next town. She might get everything of value from her car. Saying that was a good idea, she was soon at her car. Putting a scarf or something around her neck, rearranging her little black bag, coming back opening the passenger door, she was getting in. Setting the little black bag neatly between her feet.

While driving down the road, she was sizing him up. He seemed harmless, 50 years of age, pretty good looking, no ring on his hand, she wondered about that, a new car, rather nice clothing, you could smell money. Those thick shoulders, arms and hands, a powerful man.

Coming around the outskirts of Aitkin, a large store, a super market on the left. Pulling into the deserted parking lot, off to the side, shifting into park, cutting the lights. Wondering, just turning when the back of his hand hit, driving her into the door. Setting stunned, nothing happening. Looking up she could see the silver pistol in his hand.

Calmly he said, "Just want you to know who is the boss, do as you are told, you may walk away. Screw up a little, they'll find you in a ditch somewhere. You understand?" Taking the key from the ignition, getting out, walking around the car, opening the door, lifting her arm, he was putting a handcuff tightly on her wrist, the other to the seatbelt, clicking it into place.

Getting back into the car saying, "Just up around the corner there is a gas station. I'll be filling up, you do anything to draw attention to us, you're dead, understood?"

Slowly she raised her eyes, looking into his. He could barely hear the "Yes" that came from her lips.

"What the hell was going on here, a chill had just gone up his spine." Looking into those eyes, he felt trapped. Then she lowered her eyes in submission. What an imagination, he was totally in control. A few days with them, she would be eating out of his hand, they always did.

Pulling into the station, he was soon filling up, occasionally looking back; he was keeping an eye on her. Taking his time, he was so sure of himself. Returning he had two large bags of groceries, a gallon of milk and two six-packs of Grainbelt beer.

Getting into the car, looking at her, he said, "Good girl", the slap had done the trick. Driving through town and keeping on 169 north, always watching his speed, he knew if there was a place in the state to get a speeding ticket, it was around Aitkin.

As they were leaving town, he said, "What's your name, don't lie to me, I will go through your purse and check you out." She murmured, "Check me out." My name is Donna Wagner, I'm 29 and live in Minneapolis, working as a nurse. I have only had a couple boyfriends but I'm sure I can please you any way you wish." She could feel some excitement in her, this guy is dangerous. Think then act, it could take a while. As she felt the necklace around her neck, cheap but priceless. Looking at him in a submissive tone, "What shall I call you?" "Tex will do." The excitement, watch yourself. Saying, "I'm thirsty; couldn't we crack a couple of those beers?" Tex didn't think that sounded like a bad idea, pulling to the side of the road. They could see the lights of Hill City. Opening the back door he pulled a six-pack out, breaking it open, taking one for each of them, bringing the others up front. Getting back in the car he handed Donna a can, she took it, opened it and took a good swallow. Opening his can and taking a mouthful, setting the can in the tray holder between them

As he drove, she asked him a lot of questions for someone who should be scared to death. What the hell, she wouldn't be able to tell anyone anyway. She did appear to be nervous, her hands were always moving, touching something, or fumbling with her necklace. Tex was starting to loosen up, telling her about himself. He had been a lawyer for some years, the same partner owning their own firm. Some time ago they had bought a small cabin north of here on Snow Lake about 20 miles from Marcelle a couple hours away. He was telling her everything; his partner would be up around 10 or 11 the next morning. She would like Dave, they shared everything. A threesome could be most fun if you know what I mean. We've been up here at least three times this last year. As he talked, he would take another swig of beer. She was matching him pretty well, always playing with the necklace around her neck. Nervous, I guess.

He was looking at her, how her breasts pushed out the sweater stretching it. The beautiful skin, just the right amount of hips. The fire in her eyes seemed to make him uncomfortable, he would tame her. His partner was going to go nuts over this one.

The three women taken over the last year had all lost it in a couple days. Who wants to screw around with a crying, sniveling woman, they had all asked for it. Now all three were resting peacefully in their shallow graves behind the cabin. When we are through with Donna she will join the others.

Tex had newer anticipated what a thrill it was to take turns with Dave, looking into their eyes, the fear. Squeezing their pretty throats until their eyes were lifeless glass. The part Tex didn't like was trying to lift a lifeless chunk of meat after their bowels had let loose while getting them to their resting place. Then the filthy cleanup, how many times can you wash your hands? He would make sure the next kill would take place by the grave she was buried in.

Donna was surprised that this was going to be so easy. They had gone through Grand Rapids some time ago. Marcelle was slipping behind. Then the turn off to Snow Lake. He said it won't be long. They were on a seldom used dirt road.

Donna was nervous now fumbling with her necklace as she was thrown against the center counsel. Something dropped from her hand into his half filled beer can. Then they were at the quaint little cabin. Looking she could see the full moons reflection off the lake. Saying out loud, "What a storybook place."

He pulled the car up into its parking space. She turned, raising her beer can up, saying, "Let's drink to a wonderful couple of days." Lifting his can, he said "I'll drink to that." Emptying the cans and throwing them into the back seat.

Then Tex was there unlocking the handcuffs telling her to carry her own things. If she wanted to run, she's better be fast as a bullet in her spine would slow her down.

Did she detect a stutter in his speech? Then he was unlocking the door, stepping in, the cabin was built for openness, very expensively furnished. In the far corner was an over-sized bed with a heavy metal framed headboard. Close by was a rollout.

Setting his luggage down, he took the cuffs from his pocket, walking to the large bed saying, "Come here."

Donna knew what he had in mind, saying, "We had been in the car a long time, I have to hit the can, do you mind?" "No," he said, "go ahead," as he sat on the edge of the bed to wait. After the long trip he was starting to feel a little groggy himself. Hearing the shower turned on, he yelled, "What in the hell are you doing in there"? Looking up, there she was a goddess if he had ever seen one, tall, statuesque and bare with water dripping from her long hair.

She said she wanted to be clean and perfect for you, stepping back into the shower. She had to take her time. The GHB a date drug she had dropped into his beer was starting to take affect. She had also dropped a small amount into his first beer. He had then become very talkative, more than he had realized.

She had recognized him when he had first pulled his car to the side of the road where she had hit the deer. The warning flags had gone up when he had given her the name of Tex Landow. She was well aware he and his partner had a law firm just a few blocks from where she worked in the Cities in the Minneapolis Police Department. She had been a detective there for some time, her real name was Sandy Dove but if she had given him her real name, he may have placed her because she had been in newspapers as the detective that solved missing women's cases. When he had given a false name, she decided to play along.

While yet out on the highway when she had gone to get her purse and black bag she had rearranged it turning on her long playing digital recorder. Tucking her service gun with her badge under some women's pads, turning off her phone. He had been so sure of himself he had never checked her out.

She had been on her way to lecture at a law enforcement meeting in Grand Rapids to be held at the Cedar Inn, leaving a day early to have the time to explore the town.

While Tex had been gassing up in Aitkin, she had quickly called Pat at home, he was both a professional and personal friend who worked as a deputy in the Grand Rapids area. Pat was the person who set up the talk she was to give at the Cedar Inn to law enforcement. She told him to record this; what had happened, who she was with, car license number and color. He was given her phone number and would attempt to follow her with GPS signals from her phone. Giving him both of the lawyer's names, he was to check ownership and location of the cabin. Having convinced him there was more going on than just her kidnapping, she could handle herself, she would try to keep him updated.

Dove then stepped out of the shower, taking a large towel, standing in the living room to towel herself off. Tex or Greg as she knew him was passed out on the bed. Walking over she removed his pistol and cuffs pulling his hands up to the headboard rail, she cuffed both hands to the metal headboard, wondering how many times they had done this to some poor woman.

Quickly dressing, it was getting close to 6 am, she still had so many things to do. She started by going through the dresser drawers. Not much in the top, but a trove in the bottom drawers. Lots of pictures of naked women on the bed, one wrist to the metal headboard. Pictures of both Greg and Dave on the bed in various poses with what appeared to be handcuffed, distressed women. The drawers also held driver's license of several women and more personal information, address and phone numbers. Enough to hang them both. She also had almost four hours of digital recording from the car. There was also a picture of three graves in the back yard. All of this evidence could be used as Dove had been forced into the house by the owner. Out back she found a couple shovels. Walking a short distance she came to a small clearing, she knew what she was seeing.

She phoned Pat on his cell telling him what had taken place and that she was safe, that Greg's partner who was part of this was due at any time. She would be waiting for him. A short time later her phone rang, it was Pat; the other party was on his way. It was her baby, handle it. They would be a short distance behind.

Dove went over standing by a window sill where she would not be seen by someone coming in. Greg on the bed was starting to stir. Shortly you could hear a car pulling up outside.

The car door slammed and an excited man came into the cabin, moving across the floor towards the man on the bed.

There was a click, a bewildered look on the man's face, turning, a woman holding a gun pointed directly at him. He started to reach in his jacket, those eyes like a snake ready to strike, slowly raising both of his hands in the air. There was something about her that said, "Go for it". A chill ran up his spine, he knew how close it had been. Then, thy heard the cars pulling up outside. Pat was walking in with the other deputies.

Detective Sandy Dove, of the Minneapolis Police Department had everything under control.

Sandy, touching her necklace, thought they would never know. "God, I love this job."

~

2
Dad, I Forgive You

Tim was the pride of his mother, the youngest of three boys. The other two were much older and very much into sports, very manly thought the father. He would brag up their exploits to anyone who would listen and sometimes to some that didn't want to.

The older boys were leaders on the swimming team, holding some records in the 100 freestyle and backstroke. One was the quarterback on the football team and the other a fullback. So, it was no wonder that he wanted the Little Guy to start showing some spunk, but the mother had been going against him of late, telling him that Tim had been showing signs of liking music. And that he was more timid than the other boys.

Tim seemed to like the water to wade in but had not taken to it like his brothers at his age; he had made no attempt to try swimming.

One day while waiting for the older two to dress after practice, he and Tim were standing by the deep end of the pool. He thought it was time for Tim to learn to swim. Reaching down, he picked Tim up, throwing him out as far as he could into the deep end. Turning his back on the boy, he started to walk to the far end of the pool. He heard some splashing and "Dad, Dad," a cough, taking his time; the boy should be to the ladder at the side of the pool by this time. Turning to look, the boy could not be seen. Thinking the kid is trying to be funny, waiting, nothing, standing a few seconds more. What the hell, he started for the far end, looking, the boy was at the bottom of the pool where he had been thrown, no movement.

Diving in, clothes and all, grabbing the boy, side stroking he soon had the boy out of the water. His wife was going to be madder than hell. Knowing artificial respiration, he started

14

right in. A minute later, Tim started to cough and came around. Then the two brothers were there asking their father what happened. Tim, coming to heard his father say, "The boy fell in and because he couldn't swim, I had to jump in and pull him out."

Tim, remembered being up in the air, landing on his face in the water, gulping water, being so scared, choking, calling for his father but he never came.

Why was his father saying he fell in, that was a lie. Getting home his father told him to go upstairs and get some warm, dry clothing and into bed.

Shortly his mother was up to see him telling him how sorry she was that he had fallen in. Remembering, he had told the boys the same thing, he knew he could never trust his father or the water again. Still shivering and frightened he went to sleep.

Tim's mother was aware after that night that Tim avoided any contact with his dad. She thought there was something but could not put her finger on it. From that night on Tim avoided almost any contact with water including the bathtub. He would take a shower but not spend the time in there like the other boys.

She had been right in telling the father that Tim had other talents, musical as well as the arts. Having leading parts in school plays, being valedictorian in his class, going on to be a respected lawyer in his home town.

Tim's brothers were playing baseball on city teams, one working delivering beer for a local company the other working for a large construction company.

Tim, when he had the time was volunteering, helping the elderly with some of their financial problems as well as being on several boards including the YMCA.

This night it was just closing time at the Y, not knowing a woman had left her three young daughters in the lobby, going to the back to get some information. The three girls thinking the water looked interesting had made their way to the deep end of the pool. The youngest reaching down to swish the water was in. Her sister grabbing for her was pulled down. The one still out of the water started screaming trying to reach to help.

Tim, as he came in the lobby door noticed there was no one there, some children's coats on the chairs. Thinking he heard a kid scream, he looked up just as a young girl fell face down into the water. She was struggling. Running through the door, he was at the pool. The girl was only about three feet out, he started to reach and that awful fear came up in him. He pulled back, the look on her face, then he was down on his belly reaching as far as he could to her hand, Then she was out of the water and still screaming, screaming and pointing down.

Looking, he could see two of them, one on the bottom, one about half way down. He could not swim, he remembered that awful time down there. The choking, trying to breathe. The fear that was choking him now, he jumped in feet first, he was by the one half way down. Reaching, grabbing the child, wanting to breathe, fighting and floundering his way to the surface. Getting her to the edge, the sister helping to pull her out.

Trying to go down to the other girl, Tim could not make it. Coming back up, the fear still in him. What to do? Climbing out, he jumped in the air as high as he could, he jumped in feet first, he was almost there. Struggling, he reached out getting part of her dress. Kicking, they reached the surface.

There were some adults there now working on the little girls, a woman reaching out for the littlest girl.

They were trained in this, he pulled himself up and out. The ambulance was there and it looked like the girls were going to make it. Thank God.

The girl's mother was there crying and thanking him. Still remembering that fear, he just wanted out.

Going home and getting into dry clothes, just starting to warm up, he heard the door bell ringing. Standing there was a much older man crying, saying, "I know you don't want me in your house and I don't blame you, but I feel like my heart was ripped out of me many years ago for what I did to you.

God, forgive me."

Turning to go, he heard his son say, "Come back, Dad, I love you."

Meeting him at the door, they both hugged and cried. Inviting his father in, they talked for an hour. Leaving, the father said, "I have to go talk to your mother."

Tim was at the Y the next morning when his mother showed up asking where he was. They seemed reluctant to say. She said, "Where is my son?" The reply was, "He's taking swimming lessons with the kids beginner's class."

Oh, and his dad is teaching the class.

~

3
Caught

Danny had always been a thief, from the time he could first remember. He would take things he did not need or even want. If it was there and he would not get caught, it was gone.

His mother or dad was no different. Take from them, not much, just enough they would not notice. Don't get caught.

As Danny was attending church he would help passing the collection plate around. A few dollars always filtered into his pocket. And if he was so lucky as to help count the money, a few more.

As he was the older of the four children he would oft times be given money to take them to a show or shopping. Always managing to make off with his portion.

In high school he was the class treasurer. He was responsible for thousands of dollars. Danny was a very bright boy, a dollar here a five there. Who was going to spend their time trying to track down a few dollars? Also, Danny was above reproach. Wasn't he often gifting money to some of the funds now and then?

Going through high school he was working at a gas station as often as he could. While working the till he was in his glory, always handing the change back to the customer's hand while talking up a storm. Not ever counting. Short .50, maybe a dollar. Now and then over the course of the day if he didn't come up with $70-80 he'd had a bad day.

A couple of times and it was always a young person had questioned the missing money, .50 or so and Dan would say, "Sorry" and hand the person the money. Don't make a stink, they always walked away happy, they had caught his mistake. Anyone can make a little mistake, don't get caught.

Danny was driving a pretty nice car; Dad is helping him not knowing he has other sources of income.

Gas costing so much nowadays, there is no reason to pay for

it. He has his own little gas station by putting a little 12 volt pump into his trunk, running a little clear plastic hose into the side of his gas filler pipe.

He has a clear 6 ft hose hooked to the pump that can be run into a car he parks next to. It is small enough to go down the filler pipe of the other car. If someone comes along, he drives off before they get close. The small plastic hose pulls out coming with him, he can't be caught. Danny knows he can't be caught. He's always been too smart for anyone to catch on to him.

Take a little bit but not too much.

Someone is always leaving their credit card behind. Of course, he helps them a little. Lay it on the counter. Talk to them and distract them. Put it aside for a while. Don't take it too quickly. If they showed up a day or two later, he hadn't seen it.

Don't use the card in his home town. Make sure that when he uses it he has on sunglasses and a high collared coat and don't park where your car license can be seen. Use for small amounts, cut it up, it goes in someone's garbage can.

Danny's had some girlfriends in the past. He always has them pay their fair share, hasn't he always heard the president say that everyone should pay their fair share? Some of them weren't too bright so it didn't bother him when for some strange reason they broke up with him.

Danny had never been caught but he could remember coming awfully close. A few years ago when he was about 16 yrs old he had a neighbor who lived close by that was a retired police officer. Walking by his house one day he saw the man in the garage. They started to talk along the way he had mentioned that some day he would like to go to school to be a police officer which seemed to interest the man who gave him a lot of encouragement.

Stopping to talk one day he asked the officer if he could work for some money as he was broke and the family needed food. As there was no work at this time he was given some money with the understanding that at the first snowfall he would be there to shovel the driveway and the back porch.

Of course, he hadn't shown up. He knew he had a sure thing going, he did show up a couple days later showing his bandaged left hand that he had injured, saying he was sorry, that he had been injured and could not use his hand. Telling how poor the family was, having to eat oatmeal almost every meal or potatoes.

It didn't really surprise him when the sucker showed up that night dropping off over $100 in groceries then taking off without being thanked. A couple of weeks later he again stopped by asking if he could get a couple hundred dollars in cash as they were going to get their lights turned off.

The officer listened intently then said he would think about it. I hadn't thought he would go so far as to check it out some way but when he came over to talk to my parents, I was out the back door real fast. I haven't been close to that man since. That was as close as I had come to being caught.

Now I'm working for the welfare department helping older people getting their finances in order, being at the right place at the right time. There was always some way running errands for them, buying food or paying bills, losing the receipts. Not much, a little here, a little there and of course they always paid extra. Some pretty good tips after telling them what he had to go through that day. But that was yesterday.

Today he was doing his thing; he was out hunting which was his passion as he loved to kill things.

Deer season opened today. He had his 30.06 with a Leopold scope with which he had killed many a rabbit and some times a squirrel. He was a pretty good hunter and this year maybe a deer.

He loved this time of year. No snow a beautiful fall day. Hunting close to the Bigfork River miles away from anyone else, knowing this area like the back of his hand he had driven his car under some conifer trees. He didn't want anyone to steal from it.

Walking a deer trail about an hour now when he saw something up in a tree that didn't belong there. It seemed pretty well hidden. Looking closely he could see it was a trail camera. Setting his rifle and pack down he started to walk around to see how they had gotten the camera where it was. Then his mind kicked into high gear. What right did they have to put a camera out here, this was his hunting grounds. This might be the price they pay. That camera is going to bring him a nice piece of change.

Reaching up to get the camera, not paying any attention, he stepped over a rusty piece of metal onto some leaves. The sound and the pain, the anguished scream that came from his throat.

"Caught", he was caught in a bear trap! The pain, he couldn't stand it. The teeth were into his leg to the bone. He laid there but the least movement sent more pain up his leg. He was crying and hollering for help but all he could hear was the wind through the trees.

He tried through all of the pain to remove the trap but the short chain was spiked into a large tree. His pack with his knife and rifle was on the ground some 30 feet away.

He knew he couldn't take this much longer. He must have passed out from loss of blood but looking down there didn't seem to be much blood there. That was good.

It was getting dark. Twist and turn as he might the pain was still there. What an awful night, it took forever. The pain was letting off some; it must be that the circulation was being cut off. Would he ever be able to walk again?

The only thing good about the trap was that it had closed with the teeth going through his leather boot but the pressure.

Laying there thinking someone would be along to get the camera and that someone was going to get sued for a million dollars. He would show him.

Looking up at the camera that he had been about to steal, he thought, "I had never been caught before." Caught in a bear trap just because he was going to take a camera. It wasn't right.

He lay there all day thinking about his past. His mind always coming back to the pain. Why did he have to endure this? He didn't deserve it. He had always taken so little, perhaps more from the older folks, they had so much and would be dead soon anyway and wouldn't need it. The day crept by, why didn't someone come?

The night had been long and cold. He hadn't dressed to lay on the damp ground. This was the second day, no food or water. He had to relieve himself, turning to piss on the ground but he had to take a dump too. The trap was heavy, turning on to his side to take his pants down. Fighting the pain he was able to relieve himself. Getting his pants back up, he was almost laying in it. Taking some leaves, wrapping them around it he was able to throw it some distance.

By this time there was no more pain in the lower leg but while he had his pants down he could see the discoloration and blue streaks working up his leg and past the knee. He was in bad trouble if someone didn't come soon. Later in the afternoon a light rain started to fall. Shivering, he was trying to pull leaves over himself. It rained lightly through the night. In the morning the sun was so welcome, how could a man endure the wet clothes, the leg. Today he really tried to look deep within himself.

Perhaps he hadn't treated others as he should have, it would be different from now on. Looking into God was something he had to do if he could get out of this.

The night came slowly, how he dreaded it. He was sure he had heard something slinking around in the brush. Something big. Falling asleep, he awoke, something was licking his face. He was screaming and thrashing.

The wolf ran off into the night. Having seen a few wolves in this area before, he had always felt secure with his 30.06 rifle in his hand but it was over there now.

Trying to stay awake, he was getting very weak. Nothing to eat or drink. This was getting onto the fourth or fifth day. Looking at his upper leg the purple was up much further. He knew he was running a high fever.

He also knew when it got dark again they would be back, only more of them. If only he had his rifle, he would end it all.

Looking up at the trail camera, he swore he would never take anything again and true to his word, he never did.

22

Caught
The camera and the trap are still there???

~

4
Alex, The Boy Who Couldn't Walk

Alex lay there trying to remember where he was. What were those things around his head and neck? He could not move. He could feel a tingling in his hands. His mouth was dry. Something was up his nose. He tried to swallow, something was in his throat. Trying to open his eyes, it was so bright it almost hurt. Where was he? Where was his mother? How long had he been here? So many questions.

Ever so slowly his eyes were adjusting to the bright lights. There was a pretty lady all dressed in white. She was very near looking at him. Gently she was saying, "Alex, Alex, can you hear me?" He tried to say yes but no words came out. Trying to nod his head, nothing moved. What was wrong? What had happened to him? Then he was back to sleep.

Awake, it was night. He could remember more. He had been in a car, it was rolling in a ditch. He had tried to hang on to something. How long ago? There was some snow and the road had been slippery. Looking out the window it looked so much like summer out there.

He could hear the ladies talking. What a shame that a young boy could end up like this. It was a miracle he had lasted the last two months. The ladies were always kind. He heard them say that there was a G tube feeding his stomach. As he was becoming more aware, it was starting to bother him that they had to be changing his diapers a couple times a day.

The words were starting to come, the restraints that had been holding his head and neck in place had been taken away. The tingling in his hands seemed to be leaving, some movement and feeling was coming back to his upper body.

He was finally able to ask, "Where is my mother" knowing that his father had left years ago. The white lady replied, "Your mother has been asking about you but she was badly hurt and in a home across town. I'm sure she will be here to see you as soon as she can."

The white ladies seem to be with him more each day moving his arms, massaging his little body, working and stretching his legs out straight. A couple times he thought he felt his legs getting warm, then nothing.

Now his upper body was starting to respond. He was getting stronger, his hands and arms were doing what he wanted them to. They had started to put him in a wheel chair. Up and down the hall, it was so good to be out of that bed. Now it was time for something called physical therapy, working his legs more and more each day. There didn't seem to be much if anything there.

Then it was some kind of braces on the knees and just standing there with a white lady on each side. Then it was shift and waddle maybe an inch or two. Then it was, "You are doing great, just five more times and you can sit down." Within a week he made it to the door. The white lady brought in a small cake with one candle to celebrate the first walk to the door.

Where was my mother, was she alright? The white lady said I was doing really well with the walker but I had to hold on really tight.

Now it was something much harder. A small set of crutches. Try as they might, I fell down a couple times with the white ladies there. Surprisingly when falling I learned to let myself go with the fall and not get hurt. They told me how wonderful I was coming along.

One morning there was a man in a white coat reading something at the foot of the bed. Talking to a white lady, saying the boy had come here in March 1943 and is doing very well. I don't know how much longer we can keep him, he may have to be transferred to a boy's home.

That afternoon sitting in my wheelchair I heard, "Alex, Alex", there she was with a cane looking weak and drained. I had waited so long. I moved my chair. She came to me hugging. We both cried. The white lady seemed to be crying too. She kept saying, "I love you, I love you.

So after a time she seemed to get more choked up. Looking down, she tried to say something, she could not take care of herself and was getting help. I was getting well and would soon have to be moved, possibly to a boy's home until she was able to take care of herself and could get a job. We would be together some day, she promised. She looked so frail, what could I say. She had always been so loving to me. There was a tightness in my throat. All I could do was hug her and try to hold back the tears that wanted to come.

Shortly she left me in the wheel chair wondering what is a boy's home. Where is it at? Would she come and see me?

A few days later two nice ladies from Hennipen County Welfare offices showed up telling me who they were and what was about to happen. They had some new clothes for me and nurses would help me get dressed. The wheelchair and walker would be going with us as well as the crutches. They also had a supply of diapers that I could put on as I had learned to do that myself.

They would be taking me to the Gene Martin Brown Home for children on Como Ave near the Como Zoo and near to Gutterson School which when the time was right I would be attending.

After a short drive we arrived at an old red brick building a block long, three stories high with a high peaked roof where I was to spend the next two years. I was put in a room with four other boys. I had a bed next to the window and was assigned a large locker on the far side of the room.

There was a large dining room down the hallway. You were expected to keep your place at the table always neat having your own cloth napkin rolled up and in place.

Most of the boys in the beginning treated me well but with some indifference, I being younger by a couple years. This went on for some time but there was one boy, Rod, that tried to be friendly. I was getting heckled some times because I had to wear diapers as I still didn't have control.

After a couple weeks, Delbert became more abusive with remarks and a few times would stick a pin in my leg to see if I would jump. Even at my age there was a feeling, there was something wrong with Delbert. Noticing most of the boys stayed away from him, he was a loner too. It wasn't always fun but at least he paid some attention to me.

A few times when I had been taken in for a check up and telling the doctors that a few times I had felt something in my legs. They had a name for it, phantom pain.

Mother came to visit a few times when she could get there. She was walking much better and was looking to get off welfare soon promising that we would be together again. How I looked for her coming in to see me.

Delbert and I were developing a strange love-hate relationship over the past year. He would do things that some times hurt or would say things to hurt my feelings but getting to know him, I realized he had no one. I had my mother. Of the hundred boys in the home, he was the most lonesome of all.

One day I was at the top of the steps next to the railing. Delbert was next to me. To have fun he kicked at the bottom of my crutch pushing it over the step. I started to fall into the railing. Delbert was grabbing, but it was too late. Going over and hitting my head and neck solidly against the railing then rolling down the other steps. Lying there, I hurt. Starting to cry, I looked up at Delbert's stricken face. Such pain, more people were there didn't know what to do.

Then I started to laugh. I hurt but I laughed louder. They looked at me; I hurt all over, not just my head and shoulders but my legs and feet. That day I ended up with my white ladies in the same bed as before.

No one could explain really explain it but now after a few days the white ladies were working me over in physical therapy. The feeling was coming back slowly, the strength even slower. I was starting to control myself in the bathroom.

Two weeks later, still with my crutches, I was back at the children's home. The doctor told me it would take some time but the fall was a miracle. It must have moved something somewhere and that I would get much better and some day would be able to be without crutches.

I had never seen tears in Delbert's eyes before but there as I walked in with my crutches we even smiled and hugged each other. But, I watched my crutches.

From that day on we were inseparable. Perhaps I was in

his mind the first true friend he ever had since arriving to the home as a toddler.

A short time later my mother showed up with all the paper work to take me to our new home with a surprise, her new husband. She seemed so happy and he smiled. I was going to like him.

But I still had a friend to say goodbye to. Mother was going to help write letters to Delbert. This we did for many years with some trips to the zoo.

~

5
Bigfork River Justice

Anna was lying in her bed, no sleep again tonight. What was she doing here? She knew the answer to that, coming to the little cabin on the Bigfork River to end it all. Enough drugs in her purse to make sure. No friends or relatives, who would notice? There had been a terrible accident two years ago. Both, her seven year old daughter, Amy, and husband had been killed outright. The drunken driver had received a three month jail sentence and eighty hours of community service.

James, her husband had always called her the Amazon woman. She had been good at any sport. They had spent many days canoeing on the Bigfork. Amy had looked to be the athlete her mother was.

The little cabin was isolated, the only way in was canoeing, four-wheeling or walking. Lantern for light and water from the river, rustic as it was, they loved it. It was on the far end of what could almost be called a peninsula as the river turned right making a four mile circle, coming back almost within a quarter mile of itself before continuing on to the falls.

Becky had been in the Gene Martin Brown home for children on Como Ave. St Paul, for 5 years, arriving when she was four years old. No one came to visit her, well behaved but not happy. Some times she felt like bursting inside. She had few friends, there was a need inside she could not explain, even threatening to run away. They had always laughed at her. Often times crying herself to sleep, dreaming of a mother who would some day come and take her away. Being nine now she knew this was never going to happen.

This was to be a special day, a dozen of the children being bussed to a Minnesota Twins game. She was looking forward to this as she excelled in sports for her age.

It was an afternoon game and seemed to stretch forever, lasting 12 innings before the Twins got a home run winning

4-3. Then everyone was pushing to leave and some of the children got separated, Becky was one of them. Being sure of herself she headed for where she knew the buses would be parked over by the trucks.

As Becky walked by she could see a man loading a baby stroller into the trunk. The shiny new car was parked some ten feet in between the trucks. As the man loaded the stroller, a wheel came rolling toward her. She picked it up, walking to the man, handing him the wheel, he reached out saying, "Thank you" and she was in the trunk. The lid came slamming down, she heard the stroller hitting the cement. Then the car was moving. She started to kick and scream, no one heard her. As she lay in the trunk kicking she realized this was going to do her no good. Thinking, I learned to play the matrons at the orphanage, what can I do here? Play along, she got very quiet.

Frank Derby, 47 years old, working in steel construction, moving from place to place depending on where he was needed. This suited him well; he was not much to look at, certainly not a lady's man. He was driven to the very young girls or boys. In the past several years he had lived in the Cities where three young girls and a seven year old boy had disappeared, never seen again. He had been picked up and questioned on the boy, nothing could be proved. He quickly sought employment elsewhere.

It had been some time now. The urge was back. He told himself this would be the last time, as he was working on a baby stroller wheel.

His parents had left him a little cabin on the Bigfork River in northern Minnesota. This was where he had had his first encounter with a young boy. He had a strong urge to go back, but not alone.

Frank had been here a couple other times so he was not surprised when the young girl picked up the wheel and brought it to him. He did take pride in how brilliant he was. No one had seen him putting the girl in the trunk.

They had been on the road five hours and were on a lonely stretch of the road in the Bigfork area. Nothing had been heard from the trunk for some time. He didn't want to go through this work for nothing. Pulling off the road and stopping the car, he got out opening the trunk. She was not moving.

Becky felt the car coming to a stop. She was scared but pretended to be half out of it. Derby was lifting her out of the trunk; she seemed to be coming around saying she had to go to the bathroom badly. He told her to go ahead. She, saying, "No, I can't go in front of you. There are some bushes just over the ditch, I can go there."

She seemed to be unsteady on her feet, not wanting to dirty up his car, he said, "Go ahead, I'll be watching you." Getting dark, she was stumbling through the ditch to the bushes. As she went behind the bushes he turned to look both ways making sure no cars were coming. Looking back he could see the girl in her dark clothing disappearing into the brush and trees. Derby could not believe this, she must have been faking. Well, he would show her that he could run too, even with his boots on. When he caught her he was going to beat the hell out of her among other things. He had run hard for the first hundred yards or so. She had disappeared in the bush. This didn't bother him, this was his hunting land. He knew every inch of it. He knew all five cabins on this little peninsula; she would have to find one of them. No one would be up here now.

After listening and searching for some time in the dark he decided to go back to his car, get his flashlight and hide the car.

Thinking, if he could not find her, he could just take off. She didn't know him, he would be home free.

It took him some time in the dark to find his way back. The trunk lid was still open, he shut it. Then he went to turn the key in the ignition, it was missing. Looking under the seat for his flashlight, it was gone as was his sack lunch and water bottle.

I'm going to kill her. She had to have gone back in the same wooded area as it was all swamp on the other side of the road.

Taking his time, he started back into the woods; this is going to take some time. I hope she didn't throw the keys away.

Becky, after hearing him going in the one direction had cut to her right, running into the river, following it back to the car. Remembering the tire wrench in the trunk, she could use this as a weapon to defend herself. She tried to start the car but couldn't. Taking the keys and putting them in her pocket, searching the car she found the tire wrench, the flashlight, bag lunch and water bottle.

During all this time she was listening intently. Thinking she could hear him floundering in the dark woods, taking the items with her she ran down the road and then back into the woods. Not knowing if he had more keys.

This time she found the river on her left and followed it. After half an hour feeling it was safe to do, she turned the flashlight on. Now she could travel much faster in the dark using deer trails. She was tired and hungry. Sitting on a log eating the sandwich, she drank some water; she hid the sack under some leaves.

A short time later she came upon a broken down cabin on the river bank. She moved on, thinking it could be 11 or 12 o'clock. She thought she could see a lantern light in a small cabin by the river. What could she do? Not trusting any man now.

Taking a step at a time, sneaking up to the window, she could see a lantern in the bedroom. She then saw a woman sitting against her pillows, not asleep, staring straight ahead.

Anna had her window open, she knew the night sounds. Someone was out there moving around the outside of the cabin, probably to come in the front door which was never locked. It could only be a man.

They were in for a surprise. Slipping into the living room, she entered a closet with a curtain for a door. There she kept a short handled spade. Grasping it, she waited. Someone had stepped through the door, stepping out; she was swinging for the head. Just then she saw it was a young girl. The only thing that saved her was she let the shovel go; it landed on the far wall.

Alarmed, she said, "Little girl, what are you doing here?" Becky dropped to the floor and started to cry, she couldn't seem to stop.

Anna finally got the poor thing up and onto her bed. Looking, she thought she must be about the same age as my little Amy. In a short time she was finally able to tell Anna what she had been through that day and how she had lived in an orphanage, how she had dreamed of a beautiful mother who would one day come and take her away. Knowing now, this would never happen.

As Anna sat there, she thought, did God send me here not to end my life but to start a new one? She had worked in the legal field knowing the ends and outs of it. Could she do something with the girl? Maybe both of their lives could start over.

She now realized she had a bigger problem. The man probably knew this area and would soon be along. How much time did they have? So much time had been wasted, he may be outside already.

Going to the bedroom, she blew out the lantern, closed and locked the window. Taking a small candle, placing it on a table, she sat Becky on a chair next to it. Not much could be seen in the room, telling her no matter what, she was not to move.

Picking up her spade, she went behind the cloth curtain. It seemed like forever, an hour perhaps, when she heard someone opening the door, stepping in.

The spade came down, missing the head. The edge cutting into the right shoulder bone, he was spinning, going down. Then the spade came down on his left elbow cracking the bones.

He could see it coming again, the pain, the flat of the shovel caught the side of his head and he was out.

It was light when Darby started to feel the pain, head shoulder and arm. He tried to move, the pain was excruciating. He was still where he had fallen.

Looking over to the talking voices, they were at the little

table having breakfast. Couldn't they see the pain he was in? They looked over to him unconcerned. The girl seemed not to notice.

They couldn't treat him this way. He started to say something, no words came out. Then, seeing all the blood around him, "You have to get me to a doctor before I bleed to death!"

Then Frank Darby making the biggest mistake of his soon to be short life, said, "If you don't take good care of me now, as soon as I can, I will be back for both of you, I've gotten away with it before."

Anna was thinking he could be right. The drunk driver that had taken the life of her husband and daughter had spent only three months in jail. This man sounds like a serial killer! Saying, "You may be right; no one wants to always be looking back! I'll be gone for half an hour to get an aluminum boat that will take you to your freedom"

Derby knew at that moment it paid to be forceful with women, it always had.

Anna thinking it was all right to leave Becky here while she was gone; the man on the floor was not able to get up by himself. Earlier she had gotten his billfold from his pocket. She now knew a lot about Frank Derby.

In a short time she was tying a boat to the river bank.

Telling Frank this was a hard thing to do as he was such a large man. It would take all three of them to get him on his feet and down and into the boat. Apparently Frank had a low tolerance for pain which made it even more difficult.

The current was swift with the river being 25 ft deep, the boat was hard to control.

Soon he was sitting in the bow, both arms hanging over his legs trying to get comfortable thinking how I'm going to enjoy coming back here when I get fixed up. Then Anna was tying the anchor rope to his leg using a bunny-loop. Next she was putting the oars in the oar locks with the oars hanging in the water; then the life jacket was tossed into the boat.

Anna reached down, taking the plug out of the bottom of the boat. Water started to gurgle in, then pushing the boat out into the river. It turned sideways in the current; he was facing them on the bank. He watched them while floating to his freedom.

He was thinking if the boat sank the anchor would take him down. If it didn't sink the falls and the rocks were only a short distance down the river. The boat would surely turn over there and he would be dragged through the rapids a half a mile.

He tried to say a prayer but none came, and then he was hollering for help. No one heard him. The total helplessness inside of him, is this how some of his victims had felt? The current was strong; the boat was filling with water as it rounded the bend.

Anna and Becky were heading up stream in a canoe to where she had left her car. Becky was stroking real well for her first time in a canoe. They were going to have to hurry back to the Twin Cities where Anna would find the lost girl, Becky, close to the ball park, take her to the orphanage and start adoption proceedings, a new life for both of them. A prayer answered.

A week later an article appeared in the Grand Rapids Herald Review.

A man had been found below the falls of the Bigfork River, legs entangled in the anchor rope, battered beyond recognition from the rocks. A car had been found that led to the man's identification. A Frank Derby, age 47, of the Twin Cities.

~

6
Just Listening

He scurries among them, this one-eyed simpleton, a small man of no strength. What's happened to him? No one knows, yet they do. The disfigured face, the burned body, a roadside bomb or one at a market place?

He's never spoken, eating only scraps left over or thrown to the dogs. His home a hole in the side of the overhanging rocks. He has been living among them for some time.

He must be a Jihadist like them. The tribe they were in had believers, sacrificing themselves. Ala Akbar, God is great.

Many a Sunni had died from their sacrifices and many more will.

At times it was noted by some, none of the Counsel or leaders were ever volunteers to be sacrificed.

Even now a truck was parked, hidden in the Hindu Kush Mountains, deep in a narrow ravine with high rock cliffs on both sides. A stream running through it with a small road, the tribes' only way in, then through the valley and out the pass.

It was a very large truck taken some weeks ago for the purpose of loading it with explosives; it was to be the mother of all bombs. When ready, it would be parked in the city of Aleppo, the country's largest city, on the busiest of all days in the middle of the market place. Nothing would go wrong; the Chosen One would set the bomb off.

When everything was ready, the truck would be driven to its destination. More explosives were arriving every day. Two cars were sitting in the tribal area some distance from the truck. The cars would be used as follow-up to the truck. After the truck explosion, emergency personnel would respond, many people would rush in to help. In a short time, they would be detonated by remote control.

The one-eyed broken man sits in his hole, no life left in him, apparently just waiting to die. He never speaks for if he does secrets may slip out, horrible secrets. So, he listens, always listens. In his mind revenge, hot seething. The Jihadist's he now lives with are going to pay. God is great for He has led the way. He has led me to this place. Every day his strength grows stronger. His thirst for revenge cannot be quenched.

So, he waits and listens. All the information he is gathering will be used against them. Hundreds will die.

Suhayd had been a Sunnite living with his wife of many years, three children, a boy and two girls. They lived a meager life in their small mud hut, always striving to make it better for the children. With some education their lives would be much brighter.

From the time he was a youngster, he always had a knack for fixing things, becoming known as the mechanic. If they couldn't come to him, he would go to them. Living on the outskirts of Fallujah, there was always work.

The family, enjoying a hot summer day, was taking their time walking around the market place, the children leading the way next to the white van. There was a flash of light, a horrible explosion, body parts were flying everywhere. The hole in the road where the white van had been was deep.

Suhayd was starting to feel the pain, a terrible pounding in his head. The upper body felt like he was being burned alive. Where was he, on his back? He couldn't feel any clothes on himself, some kind of blanket covering his face and body. The pain was becoming more unbearable. He was trying to move, to make a sound, nothing. As he breathed, the flesh on his upper body felt like it was coming apart.

He was able to move his hand, something was in his eye. Moving his hand up touching the eye, there was a hole where the eye should have been, nothing. A couple strings hanging out, he had to know. Carefully through the pain, reaching the other eye, it was there. The eyelid was closed in blood; he could see a faint light. Such pain.

There was a ringing in his ears, what were they saying? They had to move all these bodies to be buried in a mass grave. Fifty-two dead, hundreds injured.

Someone was standing over him, his feet were being lifted, hands were biting into the burned flesh under his shoulders.

A terrible scream came from somewhere. They dropped him. The cloth was taken from his face. Someone saying that this one's alive, he would be better off dead.

Through indescribable pain, he was taken to what they call a hospital ward. Blessed were the many times he would go unconscious. Weeks going by, his strength was starting to return.

One time looking into a mirror, this was the last time. An old man looking back at him, grotesque; one eye, hair on one side of his head, upper body and face disfigured, not human.

It was like the family never lived. All traces wiped from the face of the earth. Never going back to his mud hut, two things were now burned into his mind; the images of his beautiful wife and children whenever he wanted. Closing his eye, they would be there.

The other, the Jihadist, who with such impunity would slaughter the innocent, men, women and children, walking away, always, "Ala Akbar", God is great: thinking they and their families were safe.

Ala Akbar, God willing, he would be seeking out these Jihadists and their families. They would pay a dear price.

He wandered the city, always listening for who may be Islamic extremists. He would be passively sitting, waiting to die, gaining massive amounts of information.

Soon he was aware of a Jihadist who liked to talk in a bragging manner of some of his exploits.

Shudayd had been listening to the man for some time; God had delivered him unto my hands. One morning the man was found, hand and feet bound in his lonely little mud shack, he had been filleted alive, giving much information.

A few weeks later a one-eyed man was seen walking on the mud road by the creek in the Hindu Kush Mountains, he noted how close and high the walls were on both sides of him.

Looking up the valley, he could understand why the Jihadst tribesmen would feel so safe. Someone would ask him a question, always he would look to the sky acting stupidly, then staring at them. In a short time he could be seen just sitting, listening, always listening for more information on their way of life.

These people were not farmers; they were controlling the drug trade through the narrow pass in the mountains, it was enormous. The five man Counsel was hording vast amounts of money, tons of drugs, yet to be moved. Some of the drugs were being distributed; this helped to keep their followers in line. There was some grumbling, the Counsel's word was law as was Sharia's Law where women are subservient to men treated as slaves to do men's bidding.

Suhayd, knowing one of the explosive laden cars was being parked next to the drug storage bunker, the other in among mud huts. Finding the drug bunker wasn't securely guarded at times, he was able to secure many pounds to be used for what he had in mind. The truck in the ravine was unguarded at night. Listening, he learned the electronic devices to be used to detonate the bombs were in the Counsel's bunker.

Setting close to the Counsel, listening, always listening, he had learned the time table of the movement of both cars and truck, when they were to be moved to the market place in Aleppo, the countries largest city, next to their largest air-port.

The Counsel sat together enjoying themselves, life was good. Having everything they could want; money, power, some of them would be moving on. A man approached them saying he was a man of God, believing what the Counsel was doing with their mass killings was wrong. He would not be a party to what they were planning. These killings must stop; this was not God's way.

The Counsel could only believe this was blasphemy and a challenge to their leadership. If they let it go, they must let the people know what happens to nonbelievers.

The man was arrested and lodged in a mud hut until their sentencing could be carried out.

There was to be a great party the afternoon and night before the cars and truck would be traveling a distance to do the work of Allah.

A young man was to be honored having been given large amounts of drugs over the last week. He was enjoying the adulation of his peers. Allah was great. He would not only drive the truck to it's destination but would have the special privilege of killing a nonbeliever before all of his tribesmen.

The evening was now here, early the next morning the explosives would be well on their way to do God's work. The tribesmen had been drinking and doing drugs for hours. A great party, one to be remembered the rest of their lives.

Now the Counsel was calling them all together. They had an unbeliever amongst them, he had been sentenced, a chosen one had been prayed over, then selected to carry out Allah's will.

The young man stood there, sword in hand, the crowd becoming silent, who could it be? Then a blindfolded man was taken from the mud hut, hands tied behind his back. He walked proudly, head high into the circle of the Counsel, then forced to his knees, arms bound behind him, head pushed forward.

The Chosen One stepped forward, at a nod from the Counsel, the sword was raised, Allah Akbar echoed in the valley. The sword flashed down, the man's head was rolling, the body seemed defiant, standing upright, blood shooting in the air.

The Chosen one at last, seemed to realize what he had done. Looking at the head, the blindfolds gone, he was looking at his father's face who seemed to blink looking at him. Turning pale, bending over, throwing up, Walking over and picking up his father's head, he walked off with it. A few minutes later a shot was echoing through the valley.

Suhayd was not idle during all of this time; he had been busy mixing large amounts of drugs in the Counsel's water bags and drinks. They would not be waking in the morning for more than one reason.

The celebration lost something after the beheading. Even though they were Jihadists, this man had been a friend. Knowing his views, they knew why he had been beheaded and why his son was used, who would be next? After a time of merry making, the Counsel seemed to be getting sleepy. Walking off to their special building in the protected hollow to their sleep of forever, he would be walking among them, sword in hand.

Now the one eyed man sat and waited.

In a short time he stealthily entered the building of the Counsel, no one stirred. Going to the wall he removed a bloody sword from its scabbard. Taking his time relishing what he was doing, the joy of it, a tear dropped from his eye. Soon he had five heads in a small circle in the middle of the room. Leaving a note saying, I will be back, I live among you.

Picking up the remote controls that would set off the explosives in the cars and truck, he was soon climbing to a much higher elevation; reaching its summit he sat admiring the valley below him. His work here, almost done.

Taking the remote marked for the truck, he disengaged the safety switch. Pushing the detonating button, it was indescribable the explosion contained between the two side walls of the pass. Going up perhaps a quarter of a mile and out both ends of the pass into the mud huts a tremendous fireball. Then he hit the other two detonators, the valley lit up even more. He could see the walls of the pass collapse; it was filled a hundred feet high with rocks. He could feel the heat from where he was sitting, his work here was done.

Someone would find the Counsel's heads and the note, "I live among you," would they sleep better from now on?

The explosion was so vast and powerful it was found on the seismometers as an earthquake.

It was seen on a satellite as an explosion of an unexplained force. The satellite picture going back to the previous day, a truck could be seen sitting at the scene of the explosion.

Iraq was claiming to the Security Council that it had to be some type of a huge bomb that only few people could deliver.

France was saying it had nothing in its arsenal of this size.

A head of state said it was a peaceful action, not an act of terrorism. We will investigate, you will know the truth. I guarantee it.

Two weeks later a hundred miles away, a desecrated, old one-eyed man was sitting amongst some Jihadist tribesmen, listening, just listening.

~

7
That's My Son

A woman walks into a Rochester hospital, the Methodist. She's on the wrong floor, entering the wrong room. She is dumbfounded. There is her 17- year-old son laying in a bed looking at her. She can't believe what she is seeing. Her son is dead; she was there when they gave him his last rites. Then with his parents' permission, his organs had been donated to save other lives.

His funeral had taken place some time ago. She had seen him. She stood there and didn't know what to say or do. She's looking at him. The boy is looking at her, seemingly wide-awake, showing no sign of recognition.

Not knowing what to do she walks to the foot of the bed. Looking at the patient's chart, his name is Tim Donovan, birth date, 3-21-1993, the same as her son, Tom. But this can't be, her son was in a horrible accident a short time ago, living only a few days.

It happened just east of Owatonna, a drunk driver had run a stop sign on County Road 1 and 24 at 11 p.m., killing one boy, Don Jonelm, age 16.

Nicky Peterson is at the Methodist Hospital in critical condition. Her son, Tom Miller, had lived only a few days. She is about to say something to him when the nurse walks in saying, "Can I help you, is he a relative? This is a restricted area." She starts to point saying, "My son, my son." She doesn't know what to say as the nurse is escorting her out of the room, saying, "This boy is in critical condition and only relatives are allowed in here at this time." She is left standing in the hall.

She has to get some answers or this is going to drive her insane. She knows what she has just seen, that is her son. She goes to the information desk, asking, "Who is the boy in 342?" The receptionist asks, "Are you a relative and what is your name?" She replies, "My name is Mrs. Jo Ann Miller and I would like some information on the boy in 342." The lady at the desk says, "I am sorry, but I don't have your name on the list. I can't give you any information. It is all privileged."

Again, she doesn't know what to do; she has come to visit the injured boy, Nicky Peterson. Realizing she has been on the wrong floor, she goes down to 242. There is Nicky smiling as she walks in the door. Then remembering, a look of concern comes over his face. Saying, "I'm so sorry, Mrs. Miller, I am so sorry. It was not Tom's fault, that guy came right through a stop sign. We didn't stand a chance."

Jo Ann, saying, "It's all right, Nicky, I didn't come here for that. I came to make sure you are going to be all right. I don't understand but God is going to do something good out of this somehow, someway, I just know it."

After a short time, she knows she should go as her mind is elsewhere. Getting ready to leave, she asks Nicky if there is anything she can bring him, saying "I'll be back soon, I promise."

She can not help herself; she is taking the elevator to Floor 3. Walking to 342, the door is partly open. There is a fairly young couple in with the boy. They are wearing green, sterile gowns. They are holding each others hand. The woman is crying, the man dabs a tear from his eye. She can't take any more; she walks away as fast as she can.

Soon she is driving back to Owatonna. I have to talk to someone, my husband, Don. It's late, he should be home. Turning into the driveway, his car is there. As she is going in, he is just sitting there lost, this had been his only child. She stands there before him, looking down. She breaks into heart wrenching sobs. He gets up, pulls her to him, holding her close. Thinking, let her get some of it out of her system. After a time, she seems much better. Thinking she is now in control, she starts telling him what she had seen. Their son is at Methodist Hospital in a bed on the pediatric-surgical floor.

Don sells surgical equipment for a living, aware the floor is used for all surgeries including transplants of all kinds. He must get her calmed down; she has always been so level headed. She does not want to listen. Finally getting her into bed, promising he will look into it the next morning.

At this time Floyd and Alice Donovan are sitting with their son, Tim, watching him in a peaceful sleep. Just a week ago they knew they were going to lose him. He had been on a waiting list for a year and a half. During that time no one had come close to being a match for a heart transplant for their son. The doctor had told them he had maybe a week or two, keep praying.

Tim had always been a very good athlete, playing high school basketball and a runner on the track team. Almost 2 years ago he had seemed to be running out of energy, not wanting to do really anything. His girlfriend had left him, saying he was a poor sport, wanting to stay home all the time.

One day Don said to his son, "Tim, I have an appointment for you. I know you don't think there is anything wrong with you but I want to be sure."

Showing up at the Mayo Clinic, Tim went through many tests going from one specialist to another. Then he had to go back the next day for an echocardiogram and other tests taking most of the day. At the end of the day, Tim with his father, was taken into a room with three doctors sitting there. Their doctor, Al Vrrella, introduced each one of the doctors to them, saying they were each experts in their field. After studying all of the tests and charts including the echocardiogram, they were all of the same opinion.

Tim was probably born with a heart condition and a lot of times this will start to show in the teen years, you will be perfectly fine until then. Then they have something that happens, A.C.M., a viral cardiomyopathy. In other words, the heart enlarges clearly with no reason and gets restrictive.

You have come to us showing sudden failure of the heart to function properly. To cut to the chase you will need a heart transplant as soon as possible as your heart is going to continue to decline and malfunction. We will be looking to put you on a list for a donor as soon as we can. Of course, this is something you must agree to; there will be lots of paper work and more testing.

Since that day Floyd and Alice watched their son slowly decline. They prayed a lot, knowing that someone would have to die to save their son. In all their waiting months, no one came close to a match as a donor. It looked like it was about over for their son.

Then unexpectedly they receive a call to come in and get prepared as it looked like they have a perfect match for Tim. He is placed in a room and all they have to do was wait for the heart to be harvested. Tim had to wait some time, then things are moving fast. He is pushed into the operating room, that's all Tim can remember. He is coming awake, what are all those tubes? I can hardly breathe; I'm so cold, those machines making funny noises. My chest hurts, the nurse saying that he is coming around, that he's going to be alright, as she is hanging some watery bags on a pole. The nurse is saying, "Tim, Tim, can you hear me?" The next time Tim is waking up, he is in a different room with his parents standing there in funny green gowns and face masks.

Tim's parents had been preparing themselves; this is going to take a long time. He will be taking anti-rejection drugs the rest of his life. After spending more time in the hospital, he will be spending months in a home close to the hospital, staffed by nurses. His parents will be able to stay there if they wish.

The doctors have told Floyd and Alice that Tim should have a full recovery, able to do almost everything he has done in the past.

Jo Ann Miller wakes up the next morning having spent a restless night feeling frustrated and disoriented. Don, her husband has been very patient with her explaining to her how they placed a letter of love on Tom's chest before the casket had been closed. Jo Ann could not be consoled, saying what she had seen time and again. Don said he would go and do some inquiries. Later that day he was at the hospital asking a lot of questions. Not having any more information, no one seemed to know what he was talking about. Going to the desk he would be asked if he was a relative and told the information was privileged.

How do you locate someone when they have over 300 heart transplants a year plus all of the other transplants? If you don't ask or have the right information, no one will tell you anything. Don had been doing this for some time now and was growing very discouraged. His wife not pushing so much but it was still eating at her.

Tim was laying in the recovery room with lots of things to think about. A couple of years ago he had been so full of energy and then it seemed he had started to run out of gas, no endurance. It just kept on getting worse. He remembered going with Dad for the checkup and what the doctors told him. A heart transplant. He was just 15 years old and you don't get a heart transplant at that age, those are for old people.

Then all of the waiting, the phone rings. Nothing, maybe tomorrow, this goes on and on. You had so much hope. You can see it in your parents eyes now. It's just a matter of time, I don't know how to talk to them, what to say. Dad is very strong but I can hear Mom in her bedroom.

The phone rings, the doctor is on the phone. We are to get our things together, a donor has been found. Tim may be in the hospital for some time. Tim is remembering all of this; his memory is coming back slowly. Remembering the time going so slow, a match, is there something wrong with the donor? Then Tim is being pushed into the operating room, he is hooked up to some tubes, he starts to think and everything fades out. He feels like he is in a dream, a very deep sleep, things are blurry, you can hear people talking, you are very cold, you're shivering, then you feel them wrapping you in very warm blankets, you can see people around you, there is a nurse leaning over you saying, "Tim, Tim, can you hear me?" Your mouth is so dry and my chest hurts.

Tim drifts back to sleep feeling like he is being lifted off the table. He hears, one, two, three, then he is on a cart being rolled down a hallway. Then, one, two, three, lift and then he is on a bed. Then being hooked up to a monitoring machine and oxygen. He's coming awake, the doctor is there and his parents with green clothes and a mask on and not saying anything.

Tim had the operation a week ago, everything in the room is kept sterile and he is making good progress. This evening a nice looking middle aged woman is in the doorway. She is looking at him in a strange way. Looking at her, he thinks he knows her, she is someone I should know. Then the nurse is in the room saying, "Can I help you?" The woman is pointing her finger at him, saying, "My son, my son." Then her voice falters and a nurse is leading her from the room. Tim is thinking, "I know her", and then is drifting off to sleep.

He has been making good progress living in a house for some time now that is set up with a nursing staff to monitor the patients. He, of course, is taking his anti-rejection drugs. Something is bothering Tim. Where did his heart come from? Whose was it? He had heard some dropped words from the nurses that it was from a young man. No one will tell him, that is privileged information. The woman in the doorway, who was she? What did she mean pointing her finger at him saying, "My son, my son, where did he know her from?"

Time is passing. Tim has been living at home now, he hasn't had any problems, the doctors say it is because of his youth. Life is returning to normal. On a Saturday in the fall, he is moving some newspapers for his father that are to be recycled in the garage. Looking down there is a picture of three boys on the front page of the Rochester Post Bulletin, a daily paper. The day was just a few days before his heart transplant. The boys were in a car accident just outside of Owatonna. One boy had died at the scene and the other two were transported to the Methodist Hospital, one succumbed a few days later. Looking much closer he can't believe what he was seeing, it's a picture of himself. Taking the article from the bundle, he put it on the workbench and sat down to study it.

Trying to make sense of what he is seeing, what he is seeing is a picture of himself, hair, nose, mouth, everything. The paper gave a description of the accident. A drunk driver had run a stop sign at some speed striking the Donovan car in the side injuring the driver and the passenger, killing the boy in the back seat. The driver was arrested for DUI. Nicky Peterson was expected to make it but will be hospitalized for a long time, Tom Miller died from injuries some time later and Don Jonelm had been killed instantly.

As Tim read, he was starting to think, he looked like him, had the same birth date, had died at the same hospital at the same time he had received his heart. Could he be looking at a picture of the boy that had saved his life? Did he have Tom Miller's heart beating in his chest? Who was that woman in the doorway?

He sat there for a long time thinking, becoming more convinced, now he had to know what was the boy like. Thinking they lost a son, it must have been terrible for them and what they are going through now?

Tim had to talk to his father, calling him to the garage on a pretext. He sat him down at the workbench, putting the paper before him, he stepped back waiting.

Floyd looked at the newspaper and was shocked at what he saw. Studying the picture of Tom Miller, he looked like his son, Tim, but what knocked the wind out of him was the birth date, 3-21-1993, the same as his son.

Somehow he knew right away. He had never told his son that he had been adopted. He knew they never split twins up if it could be helped but there it was right in front of him. Tim and Tom had been identical twins.

Turning to Tim, "I know what you are thinking and I know you are right. Having read all the information in the paper, there is just too much to be a coincidence. I want to look into this properly, I'm going to take a weeks vacation to do this but you aren't to say a thing to your mother until I say so."

The next day Floyd was out of the door early as though going to work. Having thought about it most of the night, he wanted to get a few more facts worked out. Then he was going to call Don Miller and see if they could sit down and talk. Shortly he was calling Don and it did not take long for them to meet.

As he sat talking to Don, Floyd laid out everything he knew. The two names, Tim and Tom, the same birth dates, the timing the heart was donated to his son, and how grateful and still feeling guilty over Tom's death. Telling him how Tim had been adopted out of the Gene Martin Brown home in St Paul almost 17 years ago. Don Miller came right out saying, "You are right about everything. Our son was adopted out of the same place. I don't think we will ever know why they were separated; it's been so long ago. But, I know this is going to be wonderful news to my wife. She had seen your son, Tim, in the hospital and thought it was our son. Tom.

At this time Floyd stopped him saying, "He is your son too, I think there is a big enough heart here for all of us."

What I would like to do is have a meeting at my house tomorrow morning and introduce our new families to each other.

And so it was.

Sometimes by giving, you receive.

~

8
The Diary

Nell, lying on her bed reading her diary, memories of the past, so many of them. She'd gotten a diary at 7. Something happened to her while she was still 5 yrs old. Something, or maybe it was someone, she never wanted to forget, drifting back to that time so long ago. She had been walking by the shallow end of the pool, slipping, she was going under. There was a young boy, Lonnie, who had saved her life. This 7 yr old boy without any thought for his own life had jumped in and pulled her to the ladder. Out of the pool standing and coughing, she was getting her bearings, thinking, I have to thank him. Looking, he was gone. No one else seemed concerned over what had just happened. Early the next day, she was back at the pool, she didn't want to miss him, she had to thank him.

At last, there he was walking in with his friends. He looked so tall and strong, his blue eyes, going to him, looking up, in her very young voice, saying, "I want to thank you for saving my life yesterday."

Grinning, he said it was nothing, walking off with some of his friends laughing at him.

That had been the start of it. Looking back she knew it could not have been love. She was too young to know the meaning. Still there had been something, a fascination. Something.

At times she had tried to hang around, only to feel he was kidded and laughed at for it. She pulled back, careful not wanting his feelings hurt because of her.

Soon, summer was gone. Nell was starting first grade at Central School downtown Grand Rapids. To her surprise, there was the blonde haired boy with the blue eyes going in to the third grade room. She smiled.

At noon hour and recess the girls would be playing Jacks and Hopscotch on the sidewalk. The boys, throwing the ball playing catch, sometimes marbles with their glass cat eyes.

One time they were eating lunch from their lunch buckets when she noticed Lonnie was sitting there without his bucket, he had forgotten it. Nell took one of her peanut butter and jelly sandwiches putting it on the bench next to him, walking away, she heard him say thanks. Her heart beat a little faster. Some times they passed each other they would say "Hi." Nell always lowered her eyes. There were times when they had been alone for a few moments, she always felt tied up inside some times finding it hard to breathe. He had always been quiet, not having much to say.

Nell kept her diary under her pillow, opening it up looking; she was startled, "Where had the grade school years gone?" She was into the 10th grade. Looking back through the diary, she could see she had been a fool, at least half the entrees had something to do with Lonnie. The last sounded like she had ogled him, 6 ft 2in, 190 lbs, blonde and two of the bluest eyes you have ever seen. What was the matter with her wasting all that time on something that would never be?

Sure, she had been out with a girlfriend, ending up necking with a guy in a car a couple times, it always ended up with them pawing her. Then her girlfriends would get mad at her because she wanted to go home.

Things were going to change. Tonight she was going to the football game. Lonnie was a standout on the team. She had never missed a game he had played in. The girls she was going with always went to the dance after the game which was held above the Village Hall in the auditorium. Buddy would be playing the trumpet, the blind woman, playing the piano. It was an exciting game; Duluth Denfield won 21-14. Lonnie had intercepted a pass running it back for a touchdown.

Nell had gone to Redding's Café after the game with her friends. After a snack they headed for the dance upstairs at the Village Hall.

This was a night she was going to enjoy, thinking back to her diary.

Nell had only been there a few minutes when Danny, a boy she had always rejected, was saying, "Is this dance mine?" Biting her lip, she nodded her head, "Yes." He hadn't expected this; soon they were waltzing around the floor.

As they danced, Danny started pulling her closer, stepping and turning, she was facing the door. Then her knees almost buckled, there he was, standing in the doorway. Danny said, "Are you alright, you look a little pale." She was saying it must be something she ate; I had better set down. He walked her over to a chair by the window, "Are you sure you are alright?" Nell said, "No-no, I'll be fine, you go and enjoy yourself."

Lonnie stepped inside, just standing there. Several girls walked up to him. Soon he was by himself. He looked her way several times. He walked her way, stopping, looking down, "Do you mind if I sit in this chair?" Flustered, she said, "No-no. Go right ahead," he sat down next to her staring straight ahead, elbows on his knees. She looked sideways trying not to be obvious. Sitting that way for some time, finally, he said, "I've got to say something even if it's wrong. So many times I've wanted to talk to you but the words wouldn't come. If you danced with me, maybe that would help."

He reached for my hand, they started to waltz, he was so rigid, stumbling, they both laughed. Nell slipped in closer, he was so tall. We started to relax.

Later in her diary, she had written, "My God, I was dancing with Fred Astair to this beautiful music, some times with my head on his shoulder. Mesmerized by those blue eyes, we never left the floor between dances. Holding hands looking at each other, wanting to get back into each other's arms. We were dancing the dance of dances. Where had he learned to dance like this? Some of the other couples were just standing, watching."

At 12 o'clock the music stopped. It was over, the magic gone. Standing there, Lonnie looking like a young kid, not knowing what to say. She couldn't lose this moment, saying, "Would you like to walk me home, I live by Blandin Beach, its pretty dark."

His eyes lighting up, saying, "I have a car, but I think I would enjoy walking with you, maybe we could talk a little."

Walking slowly by Central School, she slipped her hand

into his, gently squeezing. Looking down, smiling, squeezing back.

They were almost to Hwy 38, he hadn't said a word. What's with this guy, what could she do to loosen him up? She mumbled, "These fall nights are really getting chilly." He replied, "Oh" and started to unzip his jacket. Nell said, "No, this will do," lifting his arm up over her shoulder and stepping closer, leaning in, this had the desired reaction, he pulled her closer.

Nell said, "Tell me about yourself, what do you do? What's your family like?"

"Well, there's not much to tell, I have an older sister, married, living in Elk River, father died a few years back, working for Blandin Paper Co. It was said he was working a raft of logs up the river. He had lost his balance going over backwards, striking his head on the logs, sinking beneath the water. He never came up. It was two days before they found him. Mother lives on a small pension. I work at the Gambles Skogmo Store on Third Street weekends and after school. We live near the airport, I think you know where. I see you ride by on your bike a lot. Now, tell me about yourself."

Nell replied, "Not much to tell, I live down by the beach, I have a little sister, Debra, 12 years old, My father works for the DNR in the forestry division, he's gone a lot, some times on fires."

Slowing down, not wanting this night to end, she said, "This is my house, the brick one." He grinned, saying, "I've known where you've lived for years." Hitting him on the shoulder, she said, "You have not."

"Yes", he said, "I've made it my business to know where you lived since you gave me your peanut butter and jelly sandwich which by this time you've probably forgotten!"

She started to cry.

Startled, he said, "What's the matter, did I say something wrong?"

"No, nothing wrong, but its 1 a.m., and I have to be in," she explained.

They were standing looking into each others eyes, she was thinking, will he? She wanted him to. Lonnie looking deep into her eyes said, "Can I take you bowling tomorrow night?" She shivered, knowing what was coming next, almost out of breath she said, "Yes." Waiting.

"Good, I'll pick you up at 6 o'clock," leaning over, he kissed her on the forehead and then walked away. She couldn't believe it, calling in a firm voice, "You get back here." As he approached, what would she do? She let go and kissed him like a boy should be kissed, then turned and ran into her house to her bedroom.

Taking her diary from under the pillow, and her pen, she started to write. Her diary was always going to be there. Memories, something she could always go back to.

Saturday at 5 p.m., her mother was saying, "What's going on, you've been in the bathroom and in front of the mirror ever since you got home from work, isn't that your best purple skirt and sweater?"

Nell said, "Nothing special, a friend of mine from school is picking me up at 6." Her mother thought, "My God, she's acting just like I did, saying, "Is it a boy, who?"

Nell, answered, "It's, Lonnie, a boy I've gone to school with for years. We're going bowling at the alley below Redding's Café, you know next to the bus depot." Her mother replied, "Well, don't be out late, there's church in the morning."

At 5:30 p.m., Nell was sitting at the kitchen table waiting, watching the driveway, then looking out across Forest Lake, starting to think, he really meant it last night I think, I'm sure he did. At 5:45 p.m., she was walking around the table, "I don't even know his phone number." She was looking through the phone book at 5:55 p.m., when the little green, two door Plymouth coup pulled into the driveway. Walking to the door, picking up her jacket, trying to breathe, saying as casually as she could, "See you later, Mom."

She was opening the passenger side door, getting in, Lonnie smiled, saying, "Hi"! Reaching for the shifting knob, he was putting the four on the floor into reverse, backing up. They were heading downtown not saying anything. He reached over, squeezing her hand, Nell thought, "Well, that was something anyway."

Parking the little car at the Deep Rock station close to the bowling alley, they were soon heading downstairs. Some of the alleys were open. They chose one next to the wall. Getting their shoes and choosing which balls to use, they had to wait a few minutes before the alley could get a boy to set pins.

Then began an evening of more admiration. She didn't think her scores were bad, reaching 185 once. Lonnie was murdering the pins, all over 200, one 285. He explained to her that he oft times set pins so got a lot of free bowling. Finally, he said, "We've had a lot of fun, let's run over to Costello's Ice Cream Parlor. I could sure use a sundae and a bottle of Coke."

Some of their friends were there dropping over saying, "Hi," then moving on to do their thing. In a short time, Lonnie said, "Would you like to leave, there's a place I would like to show you, it's a place I like to go when I want to be by myself. She nodded her head up and down. Smiling, he was taking her hand, walking to the car and opening the door for her.

They were driving along the Mississippi River toward Cohasset, coming to the top of a high hill, making a left turn into the parking lot at the Federal Dam. Parking on the far side, pulling the emergency brake and getting out, he said, "This is it." Coming around opening the car door, helping her out, reaching into the back seat he took out a large folded blanket. Taking her by the hand, he said, "Come with me, I've never shared this with anyone."

Walking along the bank next to the river, perhaps 150 feet, leading her down a slope a short ways, flipping the blanket out onto the bank, he sat down.

Reaching for her hand, she was sitting next to him. Lying back, you could hear and see the raging river pouring through the dam. It seemed to be fighting itself, an unstoppable force as it went by. Looking up, a full moon breaking over the tree tops onto the raging river reflecting its golden beauty as if from a million broken mirrors and yet in its thunderous roar there seemed to be a siren call, something beckoning, calling.

Looking at Lonnie in wonderment, what was happening,

why hadn't she seen these things before? Looking up to her, he quietly said, "Now you know, this will be our place forever." Drawing her to him, he gently kissed her, laying her head on his shoulder.

They lay for some time; feeling an awakening in herself, something she couldn't explain. It was powerful; she started to shake feeling a little scared. Turning, he said, "Are you cold?" It was getting dark. "No," she said looking into those blue eyes. She couldn't help herself, reaching up, they were kissing, this was no kiss like she had ever had necking in the backseat of a car with some kid.

Feeling those arms around her, the intensity, she was responding. They could feel every part of their bodies against each other. The fire in this man, a building desire drawing her closer, desires you don't talk about. You feel almost like an animal it's so strong.

Suddenly, he was getting to his feet, helping her up. They were both breathing hard, saying, "Nell, I have wanted to kiss you forever but I have too much respect." Putting her fingers over his mouth, saying, "No-no, I wanted you too, we're going to have to be more careful, OK?" He nodded his head. Nell, thinking she'd never felt this way before, if he hadn't stopped, she knew.

Folding the blanket, taking her hand, saying, "I'd better get you home, it's late." They both looked at the raging river reflecting it's golden beauty as they were turning walking up the hill. Nell was thinking, "Something for my diary, a night that would never be forgotten."

Driving home, not saying much, both of their minds in deep thought. Walking her to the door, he said, "Thank you", taking her in his arms, a lover's kiss. Was that a curtain moving? He said, "I'll call you." She was exhausted; still she pulled her diary out to write.

"The emotion in me tonight was like that raging river, so beautiful yet almost unstoppable. What is it about this young man that is drawing the fire from me? Do I dare write this in my own diary? I have dreamed a dream, a thousand times and tonight a thousand dreams came true and if I dream a thousand more, they will always be of you."

Nell was up early the next morning, an early Sunday morning service. At breakfast she had seen her mother looking at her, a knowing smile on her face.

Getting home from church, the phone rang. Rushing, trying to beat her little sister, it was Lonnie saying, "If you're free this afternoon, I'd like to take you for a ride to show you one of my passions. If so, I will pick you up at 1." Nell said, "It sounds like fun."

As soon as Nell was in the car, he drove to Beckfelt's Gas Station on the corner of Hwy 38. Checking the oil and filling the gas tank. Using his gas coupons, he paid for the gas. They were driving south to Nine Mile Corner, making a left onto the dirt road, neither of them saying anything, content to be with each other. Finally, he was stopping on the road next to a farm that had a large swayback barn that had seen better days.

He explained his fascination for old barns; having imagined the families that had lived on these farms so long ago. He had a book of pictures at home taken with his Brownie camera. This was fascinating but she was starting to think he wanted to say something and it wouldn't come out.

Making a turn on the road next to a cornfield, he drove into some tall grass and then stopped next to the corn. Turning, taking both of her hands, he pulled her closer kissing her gently. Sitting for some time seeming to build his courage, then he said, "I didn't think things would go like this. You know there is a war going on and a lot of my friends have gone. I'm old enough to enlist so I have. I'll be leaving in a week; my parents are the only ones that know."

"I haven't gone to the dances often. The other night I felt lonely going upstairs. But seeing you sitting by the window, I was drawn to you. All I was going to do was ask you to write me while I'm gone. I had no idea these feelings for you could run this deep and I have no right to expect anything since I will be gone for so long, I'll be leaving in a week."

Nell sat there stunned, not able to move, her world was crashing down. They must have sat there for 10 minutes, him looking at her. Then he said in a subdued voice, "I don't blame you, I'll take you home."

Reaching to turn the key on, her hand was on his stopping him, there were tears on her cheeks. She moved his way, saying, "I have waited so long."

Arriving home, she had gone to her diary. Writing, "We controlled ourselves but the windows on that little coup sure fogged up." Hugging the pillow, imagining, she drifted off.

The next morning, she told her mother that Lonnie had enlisted and would be leaving soon. She had promised to write him. Her mother listened, just smiling.

The next week was hectic for Nell, the Rialto Theater one night, the roller rink, perhaps Redding's Café, a drive to see a barn in the country, always ending up at the Dam. The moon was still slashing through the tree tops, reflecting its rays upon the troubled waters.

They had gotten in late their last night together; Lonnie would be leaving on the 9 a.m. train for the Cities. Reading from her diary, reliving that night, they made promises to each other. Then he surprised her, he placed a beautiful golden promise ring on her finger. It fit perfectly. Saying, he just happened by Salmela's, you know the little watchmaker's place and saw it in the window. He promised to write often.

At 8:30 a.m., the next morning, his mother with him at the Depot, he stepped back as they said their good-byes. And like that he was gone. She walked home, feeling lost already. There was no way to write until she had an address. She checked her mail every day.

Nell started reading the newspaper to see how the war was going. Like most people she had listened to the radio and had known about the attack on Pearl Harbor that had taken place a couple years ago. She hadn't paid much attention, now she read everything.

Two weeks had gone by, her first letter arrived. Running to her room, opening it, there was a picture of Lonnie in his Army uniform. He looked so handsome. Reading the letter he left nothing out, how he missed her, wanting to see her again and talking about their future. And so it started, writing back and forth every few days, baring their souls only as lovers can do.

He was telling her how brutal the training was, 17 mile hikes with packs on their backs, learning to shoot rifles and machine guns. The weeks were flying by. Nell was sending the letters to a P.O. Box, Camp Carson, Colorado.

How excited she had been receiving a call, the operator asking if they would take a collect call from Lonnie, Camp Carson, Colorado. They had talked for 20 minutes, saying he would be getting a couple weeks leave before being shipped overseas. He would let her know, saying, "I love you," before hanging up.

Coming home, she could hardly believe it! Her feelings went into her diary tonight; she had to put them down.

A few days later, the operator was again asking, "Take a call from Lonnie Larson?" And Nell said, "Yes!" At first, they were stumbling over each other, trying to say too much too fast. Then he was saying, "You first, tell me what you have been doing besides writing letters!"

He told her he would be arriving on the Greyhound Bus at the depot at 10 a.m., Thursday morning. He would have a little over two weeks and would be reporting back to be shipped out from San Francisco overseas, not knowing where. Lonnie told Nell of how much he missed her and could hardly wait to hold her. Then he had to get off the phone as there was a line of soldiers waiting their turn.

Thursday morning, Nell was out of bed at the crack of dawn. Looking out across the lake and seeing her morning star just above the horizon. This meant good luck; she had always known it was there for her. It was going to be a long morning, she wanted to wake her mother who lately had been going around the house, like she knew a secret.

As the men would be working, Lonnie's mother, Nell and her mother would be meeting the bus at 10 a.m. Nell was dressed and ready at 9:30, and they were on their way. Arriving at the Depot, they walked inside to wait. Nell, constantly was looking at her watch, like it might have stopped.

At 10 a.m., the bus was pulling into the alley, parking by

the side door. The door opened, the people starting to unload. There he was, so tall in that uniform. Looking, she could hardly believe he had put on 20 pounds and had matured so much. Off the bus he went directly to his mother, hugging her, smiling. He looked at Nell, going to Nell's mother hugging her, saying, "How nice to see you again." She was waiting, when he turned, she was in his arms, the mothers had turned, talking to each other.

At noon both families had lunch at the Marlon Café, then Nell and Lonnie were finally by themselves in the coup driving out to the Federal Dam. Parking, looking at the raging river then slowly turning to look longingly at each other. Reaching out, their hands touching then they came together. It was some time before she could catch her breath.

Later, they were making the rounds, one family and then the other, talking to a few close friends. That evening they were watching Gone with the Wind at the Rialto Theater. Costello's Ice-cream Parlor came next. The little coup was heading west toward Cohasset.

At 1:30 in the morning, Nell, getting out of the coup quietly slipping into the door. She was about to knock on her parent's door when mother came out shutting the door behind her. Taking Nell by the hand, walking across the hall into Nell's room, sitting down looking at Nell who seemed to be glowing, saying, "Would you like to talk?" Nell tried to say something, then it came out, "Mom, he asked me to marry him." "What did you say?" She was trembling. I said "Yes." "You know you just turned seventeen, you have your schooling and so much ahead of you. When does he want to marry you?" Nell looking her mother in the eyes, said "Tomorrow, we can't wait any longer, it's going to happen. I know you won't and can't understand this, but there has always been something between us."

Nell's mother knew what her daughter had said to her about waiting and it was going to happen - daughter like mother.

Nell's mother told her a secret that night, how one day she had come into Nell's room to straighten up, a diary lying on the floor, picking it up, she started to put it under the pillow. On impulse she looked at the first entry, it was about someone saving her life when she was very young. She had also read the entry about the raging river reflecting its golden beauty as if from a million broken mirrors, its serine call, his refusal to go further.

"Your father loves you and at first will be against it but I'll take care of him. Now about tomorrow, could we put it off one day? I have a beautiful white wedding dress that could be ready by Saturday, it will fit you perfectly."

Turning the page: Pictures being taken, the parents standing back proudly, the bride and the groom, her in the white wedding dress, him in his 1st Class uniform on the banks of the Mississippi.

Then it was over to Forest Lake Lodge and the gathering of a few friends. Some cans had been tied behind the little coup, "Just Married" with soap on the trunk.

Nell was in the bathroom with her mother saying, "I'm a little nervous, is there anything I should know?"

Her mother said, "Honey, he's your husband now, you two will work it out," Dropping her head, she added, "Just make sure he gets a little rest!"

A short time later they were driving west on Hwy 2 past the dam. Before Cohasset they made a right hand turn onto Hwy 62, a few turns later a sign could be seen, it said, "Back of the Moon Resort." Pulling into the resort there were several quaint little cabins along the shore of Bass Lake. Parking before Cabin No. 4, he was around opening the door helping her out. Taking her hand leading her up the steps to the door, saying, "This is our home for the next couple days." Leaning down he gently kissed her, she was off her feet being carried through the door.

It was well after midnight when they decided perhaps they should get their things from the car. That was good as for some reason; he had forgotten to turn the car off.

Early one morning, sitting at the table writing in her diary, thinking, "Where had the last couple days gone?" Looking out across the lake on the horizon there was her morning star.

She thought, that's what we were like. Two stars colliding, we couldn't get enough of each other. Her eyes went to the bed, Lonnie her husband, sleeping so peacefully. He did look a little tired. They would take the time today to walk the beach and explore the resort.

Walking over, taking off her robe, she slipped quietly into bed, laying her head on his shoulder. He hardly stirred, saying, "Just a few more minutes." Nell laying there thinking, live for today, you don't know what tomorrow may bring, but she did. It was going to bring separation; it could be a very long time the way the war was going. She snuggled in closer, tears starting to come, quietly praying to herself and her God.

Driving into Nell's driveway where they would be spending the last couple days, both parents and Deborah were there to welcome them. There was some sitting around talking, then Nell and her mother were in the kitchen. Nell, you have bloomed into such a beautiful young woman, the swimming and walking the trails at the resort may have taken a couple pounds off Lonnie." Nell smiled and said, "Thanks, Mom!"

Then it was "goodbye" all over again, only this time it was at the bus depot. The parents said their good-byes, going into Redding's Café leaving the two alone. The bus was there a few moments, then it was gone.

Nell came to them with a set jaw knowing it was going to be a very long time.

The next word from him was on a penny postcard. They would be boarding ship in a couple hours, saying he loved and missed her, it might be some time. There were a lot of X's along the bottom of the card. In the meantime she would be writing every few days.

Nell was reading the newspaper and listening to the radio trying to keep track of what was happening. Every month or so she would get a letter from Lonnie, sometimes parts would be cut out of the letter. Sometimes, half of the letter would be inked out. The sensors were always afraid some secret information would get back to the enemy. There were billboards saying, "Loose Lips, Sink Ships".

At times there would be rumors the war was just about over. Sometimes, she would be reading about the Battle of Britain, what had happened at Bataan or about MacArthur in the Philippines. One that really stood out was raising the flag on Mount Suribachi on the Black Island of Iwo Jima. Some of these boys were brought home to sell war bonds. Ira Hayes was one name she could remember; Pima, a Native American Indian. The letters came less frequently, she prayed, ever fearing she would never see her husband again.

Nell, upon her graduation from high school, looking to the future, had entered a nursing program and was now a registered nurse. She had been so proud when writing Lonnie of her graduation not knowing if he ever received the letters.

There were entries in her diary, the Germans had surrendered at Potsdam in May of 1945. Could the Japanese be far behind? Some months later, there was word two atomic bombs had been dropped on Japanese cities, one Hiroshima, August 5 and on Nagasaki, August 9, 1945. Japan surrendered unconditionally.

There were parties and singing in the streets. Nell took no part in them. Hugging her mother she went to her room and had to cry. Lonnie would be coming home in one piece.

Nell received a letter a couple weeks later, Lonnie said they were breaking up some of the units, hoping to be home soon.

Two months later, Nell received a phone call from Lonnie; they had just disembarked from their ship in Seattle, Washington. They would take a train to Camp Carson, Colorado to be discharged, hoping to be home in a couple weeks, probably by bus. She was writing in her diary, laying there thinking about Lonnie, what were some of the things they would do? Turning back the pages to that first night they were married, that quaint little cabin. Thinking back, her face turning red. They would have some catching up to do.

Time had been dragging; he would be on the bus at 2 p.m. Parking the car at 1:30, and for once the bus was early coming in at 1:40.

Waiting at the door, a young man in uniform stepped off the bus. She almost stepped back, what had they done to him?

He looked like he had lost 30 lbs. He was dark; he looked to have aged ten years.

Nell was walking to Lonnie, reaching out, their hands came together. He looked so grown up and serious. Standing and looking into each others eyes, then with a sigh, he was pulling her close, saying, "Many is the time I thought I would never hold you again." He was hugging and kissing her, she could feel the hunger in this man, she was responding. They both stopped. Looking around, out in the open they felt a little silly. Walking over, picking up his duffle bag, it went into the back of the little car.

It was getting into October with a chill in the air. He had to turn the heater on to warm the car. He loved his winters here; it was good to be home. They had already made arrangements for a nice room at the Rainbow Inn. It had a large pool, was kept very clean and an adjoining dining room.

Nell was working at the Itasca Memorial Hospital next to the river, this would be a vacation week for her. They were driving to Nell's parent's house to pick up some of her things. Both families would be dining at the Rainbow tonight.

Nell's mother, Maria, and father, Ted, were both very gracious, giving him a hug. He thought, my, how Deborah had grown, she was becoming a beautiful girl like her sister. A short time later they left to meet Lonnie's mother, Jan. Driving in, she was standing in the doorway, waiting for her son, her many prayers had been answered. She hugged and cried, finally stepping aside so they could enter. Then she was hugging Nell who had been over to visit many times and to share her letters while her son had been gone.

Nell was sitting back taking it in, two wonderful families. Her husband so gaunt, she was going to feed him, put some weight back on him. Their room was just down the hall next to the swimming pool. She knew she was blessed. At 8:30, Ted said he had to work in the morning and would be getting up early. Jan said she had the early shift as a waitress at the Marlon Café. They bid each other good-night.

Nell and Lonnie were left sitting alone. They looked at each other, Nell said, "Should we?" Stopping to look at the swimming pool, then hurried on, the pool not in their thoughts. About midnight they sat up in bed and started to talk. In the dim light she ran her hand over a 10-inch scar on his right chest, saying, "What is this? You never told me you had been wounded."

Not wanting to talk about it, he was about to find he hadn't married a wimp. This left him no choice. He and some of his men had met a Japanese bonsai charge taking a hill; a bayonet had cut across his chest, through his jacket not going very deep. He was back with his outfit in a couple weeks.

Then she told him about her job, the money she had saved from his army allotment, her parents wouldn't accept anything for her living there. They would be staying there until they had a house or apartment of their own.

Lonnie told her he planned to school under the GI Bill, having always wanted to be an electrician. The pay was good. There was always work. He could be going to school and work part time, saying, "We're very sound financially."

Nell was up early the next morning, her diary before her. They had a wonderful week together; the swimming, talking, so much to catch up on. Now back to the real world, getting their things together.

Nell's mother was the only one at home when they returned. Ted working and Deborah at school. Greeting them with open arms, Lonnie said he would have to drop down to have a cup of coffee and talk to his mother.

The coming weeks were busy. Nell with her work at the hospital, Lonnie setting up his schooling. He had contacted the VA about the GI Bill.

Many years passed and Nell was lying on her bed very confused going through her diary. Lonnie, a war hero coming home 40 some years ago, successfully went to school to be an electrician and now had his own business, Larson's Electrical Contractors.

Nell thought about the daughter they had who reminded her of herself, always in her heart and diary. Looking back through all the years, she knew she had lived the life of Cinderella. Nothing could ever take from her the love she had for this man who had once told her their love forever would be entwined to the very end. Nothing would ever separate them. It started the day he had taken her to the ladder so she could climb out of the pool.

These years had gone so fast. Something was troubling her. She seemed scared and confused. This morning putting the silverware into the drawer, she found herself putting the spoons in the forks, then the knives in the---she couldn't figure it out. Then finally leaving them all together.

Last night she had gone to the bathroom finding herself in the living room. Going back to bed not knowing which side to get into.

She was starting to think back, why hadn't she noticed this before? A month ago she had gone shopping, getting home almost an hour late. She had been to the L& M Store in the eastern part of town and couldn't make up her mind which way to home.

A week ago she had jumped on Lonnie for leaving his shoes by the door, she had stumbled over them. He had always left them there. She had noticed the funny look on his face. She had never raised her voice like that to him.

She was starting to look back as much as a year, the lost car keys, missed hair appointments.

Laying the diary down, getting a pencil and paper, she started to write a list. As she wrote, more instances were added.

She stopped, she was sure, having been a nurse. Picking up the phone trying to act composed, she called Lonnie to come home. They were going to talk.

Lonnie walked in the door, he had a troubled look on his face, she could read it, he knew.

The tears were starting to come to their eyes. Taking him by the hand, she led him to the couch. Looking into his eyes, she asked, "How long have you known?

He just sat there, this big strong man, jaw tight, tears ready to burst forth. She reached over and gave him some Kleenex. Then he was leaning over, head in his hands, shaking uncontrollable sobs, trying to control himself.

Looking at him, thinking, how long had he carried this terrible burden trying to protect me? Then she was pulling him to her, letting him get it out, she could wait. They sat on the couch, arms around each other for almost an hour, never saying a word. Then very quietly she said, "How long, tell me every thing."

Looking into her eyes, he said, "Possibly a year and a half, possibly two years. A year ago, on your checkup, the doctor had said he thought it was pre-senile dementia or early onset Alzheimer. Up until lately you had been doing so well."

"I've talked to doctors, read books, thinking there must be a cure; I found there is no treatment, no cure," he explained. "There are drugs you may need; you're not ready for them yet. How much time you have, no one knows. It's all a day at a time, it could be years."

"I'll always be here for you, I have sold the business, we'll be free of it," he continued. "When the time comes, there is the Golden Gates Assisted Living here in town. We would have our own rooms and nursing care as needed.

"I'm so sorry; this has been tearing me apart trying to protect you until you had to know."

"Lonnie, my love, listen, I'm a nurse. I know what a horrible disease this is and what happens to people, but locked deep in my heart, you are. So, if you ever look into my eyes and see nothing, look deeper and listen, every beat of my heart will be saying, I loved you."

Now there was nothing that should be said, Lonnie, getting off the couch, picked Nell up, carried her to the bed and laid her down. She placed her head on his shoulder, he put his arm around her. Her safety, her protection, soon she was in a peaceful sleep. He was at peace drifting off.

That evening she was writing in her diary, writing words of love and endearment and thankfulness while she could still express herself to him.

The next several months she could feel herself slipping further from reality. Like a fog, she fought so hard but there seemed nothing to hold onto. Sometimes she was there.

A birthday tomorrow, getting ready, finding the party was

a few days ago. Where had those days gone? Looking, he was there always, so tired.

The next morning she was coming from the bedroom, when she heard Lonnie on the phone telling someone they would be moving the next day into the assisted living complex. He desperately needed the help; bathing, feeding and cleaning her after the bathroom accidents. He could no longer keep track of her all the time. Last night the fire alarm had gone off in the kitchen, he had rushed in; there was a towel on the stove on fire. She had put a kettle on the stove on top of the towel to boil, turning the burner on high.

As Lonnie talked, Nell realized he was talking to their attorney, Gene Turner, trying to get all of their affairs in order, saying he had seen his doctor for chest pains. Having been checked, he was told it was nothing to worry about. He would be over in a few days to sign the papers.

Later, Lonnie came to their bedroom. There were tears in her eyes while she was trying to write in her diary. Nothing was going on paper. She had the pen upside down. Leaning in close, he pulled her to him. This would be their last night in the house they had built together. She had been his everything as he built. The house would not be sold, as they would wait to see what the future holds.

The next morning, loading the van with what would be their needs, clothing, their wedding picture, some knick-knacks. If they needed more, he would be back.

Their Golden Gates rooms were quite large. A spacious living room area, a bathroom, a large bedroom, on each side of the room a large bed. Their choice to sleep together or apart. A dining room was down the hall a short way with set times to eat. Two nurses were on duty at all times and four LPN's. There were phones, TV and a buzzer if you needed assistance.

Moving had been a blessing. There was some help; he still thought she was his responsibility. As time was passing, she was slipping further away. At times smiling like she recognized him, then off into nothing. Then he remembered - laying for some time listening to her heartbeat, it said, "I loved you." She was still a beautiful woman, the one he had always loved.

Months were going by. Looking at all the staff around him, Lonnie realized he couldn't remember any of their names. A young lady had come to visit, he didn't know her. She had been here before.

He could remember Nell, she was his wife, even though she didn't know him. He had been so intent on her, he didn't realize what was happening to himself. He felt he wasn't as sharp as he should be; he went to the desk asking, "How long have we been here?" He was told three and a half years. It couldn't be, he thought. But it was. He had to sit and think. Going to his room, he had trouble finding it. Sitting, holding Nell's hand, he thought about his promise that he would always be there for her so he wrote himself some notes, hiding them under his pillow. They seemed to help. Then he was taking his sleeping pills and saving them in a white bottle each night--- in case?

Lonnie was sleeping one evening when two night nurses came into the room. Silently walking to Nell, they picked up her arm, feeling her pulse, then her forehead, whispering it was her time, perhaps a few hours. One of them said a relative had been called in California this morning not knowing if she could make it.

At 1:30 a.m., a young lady walked through the door. Lying in the bed was Lonnie with Nell's head on his shoulder. On his chest lay the diary and a wedding picture. Walking over, she looked down at them knowing they had been gone a short time. A nurse stepped in the door and left.

The young lady stood there for some time, then reached over and picked up the diary. She knew there were many references to her in it, knowing where to look for a special one. Here it was: Born to Nell and Lonnie Larson, Aug. 4, 1946 at 5:30 a.m., Beth Morning Star Larson.

She had been lost to both of them years ago, they now had each other. With the diary, she would keep them close.

Taking the diary, the picture and the little white bottle, she thought, heart attack, and walked from the room.

A month later, if you drove by the graveyard early this Sunday morning, you may have seen a young lady, Beth Morning Star, standing in a blanket of snow reading off a large black, onyx headstone.

It read: He brought her to the ladder, they are now climbing it together.

Beth looked to the star on the horizon and then walked to her husband and three children waiting in the car.

~

9
The Fighter Pilot

Here I am, the great fighter pilot, Bob Christensen, born in Shovel Lake, Minn., in 1928 trying to follow a dream - learning to fly a Cub Airplane off my father's grassy field just off the side of the barn. It had taken some time, Dad thought I was doing fine for my age. Teaching me how to go high, climbing, climbing to put her nose in the air and into a stall. Then as it dropped over kicking the rudder over and the stick, bringing her out of a stall. Flying pylons, learning to bring her into beautiful touch downs. Bringing her in without a bounce, just smooth on a short, narrow grass cow pasture.

It had been my dream to fly for the US Army Air Force since reading about a pilot from Hill City that had gone on to become one of the greatest Aces of World War II, Donald Beerbower. He shot down 17 German planes before being killed, shot down over a German air field while leading his men on a raid.

There were a few times I caught hell from Dad for tearing some of the fabric on the plane while getting too close to the barb wire fence. But I had to repair it even if it took a week and no flying until it was repaired, with Dad inspecting.

The dream I had was a thing I could not shake, wanting to go into the Army Air Corps as soon as I graduated from Hill City High School. But Dad insisted I take at least two years at a junior college in classes that would help my career, possibly getting me into Officer's Candidate School when I joined.

Something I really enjoyed was going to the Grand Rapids Airport taking some flying lessons from Ned Powers and Lefty Frizzell. Ned Powers was a great flying instructor having checked out on almost everything there is to fly. You try to learn from the best.

In 1948, I joined the Army Air Corps, first getting into preflight school then onto flying school. Learning to fly the trainers first then I moved onto more advanced aircraft like the P51's, P38's and multi engines while living my dream of becoming a fighter pilot. Becoming commissioned a 2nd Lieutenant upon graduation, I thought I may someday be flying one of those jets that were being built and tested.

Then in 1950 North Korea invaded South Korea. Thinking this was what I had been waiting for, I would soon be in the thick of it. Little did I know.

The next thing I knew I was in Florida flying a Cub (a Cub is about as small and slow as an airplane can be), practicing as a spotter for a 155 Howitzer. The 155 Howitzers are large guns shooting up to five miles generally sitting behind frontline troops a distance forward. Spotter airplanes call by radio telling the 155 where to shoot.

After several months of this training, I was not too happy, but then received my orders and on my way to Japan. After a week, I was flown to Puson, South Korea with orders I would be attached to the 3rd Division as a spotter for a battery of 155's.

A short distance behind the battery, a small airstrip had been cleared for five small spotter planes with some tents for the ground crew and pilots. Off to the side were barrels of gas for the planes. The planes were up most of the day, weather permitting, either looking for targets or gathering information.

If troops or vehicles were moving beyond the range of our 155 Howitzers, the spotters would call headquarters with that information and they may send in the Marine Corsair prop planes with 50 caliber machine guns and rockets called Gookgoosers or Napome bombs.

I had been spotting for some months now having given up on ever getting into a fighter plane but I was getting to be a believer that flying my small plane was saving lives on the ground below. Several times, I was directing 155's to bring down their large explosive shells on groups of enemy soldiers that were threatening our men, some times killing most of them or just clearing the way so our men could move. More than once, I came back with small holes in my wings, once almost losing the plane when an oil line had been shot through.

One late afternoon having seen North Koreans in a line half a mile long covering the side of a hill about 10 miles into their territory, I was wondering what was going on. As I flew over the hill I could see nothing. However, as I cleared the next hill there was a flash. Looking down, there appeared to be a man swinging his arms with something reflecting the sun. He appeared to be alone, possibly an American.

I thought if I dip down too low I might give his position away. Thinking more about what to do and marking his position, I circled several hills low, even drawing fire from the North Koreans. Then I circled back where I had seen the man with his reflecting plea for help. Going over him at around 200 feet, it was a G.I. It was starting to get dark, not much I could do now. Getting up high I could see what the terrain was like - mostly hills. No place to land. Looking off about three miles, I could see a small road. Taking my note board and paper, I drew a map where the sun was setting and the little road with instructions telling the soldier I would fly over the road just after sunrise the next morning. If I could see a signal I would land. He would have to be ready in 2-3 minutes on the road and we would be moving. Taking my coffee thermos, emptying it, I put the instructions in it. Circling a few hills, I hoped the enemy wouldn't see it as they were only a couple hills away. I cracked the door, spotting the reflector and coming over low, I dropped the thermos bottle. I should have been a bomber pilot. It looked like he had to duck to have it miss him. Then gaining altitude, I flew off to have a better look at the road. It was quite narrow. Then to my surprise, there appeared to be a gun emplacement about a mile down the road.

Getting back to my small air strip, I went to the captain in charge telling him what I had just seen and did. To say the least, he was not a happy man. We could not leave one of our own if there was a chance to rescue him.

Somehow it had slipped my mind to tell him about the gun emplacement down the road. I also worried that there was such a small area to get the man in quickly and not much power to get off the ground fast with the added weight.

Early the next morning, doing a preflight check, standard procedures, I told my ground crew to only fill the tank half full to hold the weight down hoping to be gone for only a short time.

Checking my maps, orienting myself, I was soon taking off for my rendezvous. As a safety precaution there would be two Navy Corsairs off a flat top high above me in case of trouble. They had the plan timetable and coordinates, I would have direct radio contact.

Approaching the hills, circling some of them randomly, coming over the road there was no sign of the signal. Had something happened? In his condition he could not make the three miles over the rough terrain in the dark. Circling a couple more times, I thought I knew what the problem might be. Flying quite high, the sun was up but down in the valley where the road was the hills were blocking the sunlight yet so he could not signal. I had to wait.

Thinking it would be a good half hour before he would have sunlight, I started to think of my half filled tanks. Leaving the area, killing time, I flew over the road at a much higher altitude. There was my signal about half a mile from the gun emplacement. Up the road a mile or so could be seen a squad of North Koreans heading to the gun emplacement getting closer to our signal. There was no time to waste, radioing the Corsairs alerting them of the situation, I told them I was going down.

I came in from high above the enemy heading in the same direction and into the wind. Going over the North Koreans a short distance, I side-slipped the plane to bring her down fast, flaring her out on that narrow, bumpy road just like at the farm.

Looking to the side were two men coming out of the rocks and brush! Two men, there was just no way we were going to get two more men into that small plane. To make matters worse, the Koreans saw what we were doing and broke into a run.

Trying to think as I pulled up to them, one was in really bad shape having been wounded. Opening the door and getting out, letting the motor run, I pulled out my chalk ropes (ropes that are used to tie a plane down at the airfield). I climbed out and threw them to the ground. Seeing the men up close I realized neither one was in good shape. We were having trouble lifting the worst of the two up and into the door. We just stuffed him into the back compartment not even facing forward. The man helping me was a sergeant. Looking in, he said that it didn't look like there was going to be room for him so he'd better run for it.

Saying, "Hell, no! We are going together," I gave him my goggles and told him to get over the wing strut with his feet on the wheel strut. I started to lash him to the strut tight with my tie down ropes. The Koreans were running and shooting behind us, coming close.

I could see the Corsairs way in front of me coming in low and fast. Climbing over the man tied to the strut, I could waste no time. Hearing him grunt as I put my foot in his back, I pushed myself into the front seat not even taking time to shut the door.

Sliding down into the seat, grabbing the stick and the throttle, I put my feet on the rudders and pushed the throttle full ahead. Hearing the Corsairs chewing up the ground behind us with their 50 caliber guns was a welcome sound. God bless the Navy!

Starting to pick up speed, the tail starting to lift, the plane was up 10 feet, then 20 feet, she would not lift fast with all the weight. Up a little higher, there I could see him standing in the road by the gun emplacement. Gun up, it could be an automatic, he was standing waiting to get the pilot. Then I knew what I had to do. Pushing the stick forward, the nose dropping down picking up more speed. You could see it in his eyes. Throwing the gun aside he started to go down. You could feel and hear a bump as he caught the wheel.

Picking up more speed we were starting to climb, but wouldn't clear the hill in front of us. Slowly banking left, we followed the road through the valley. After gaining some altitude, pulling the throttle back just enough to keep us up there, we tried to give our outer passenger a little relief. He did not look very happy from what I could see. I hoped the goggles helped.

Looking at my gas gauge, I just prayed that in about 20 minutes we would reach our destination. Having called in, they had an ambulance standing by not taking any chances and with the tank reading "empty."

There was our little grass strip. Coming in, over weighted on one side with some drag, this had to be a good landing.

Coming in, holding her off, cutting the engine, a little left rudder. A perfect landing, just like next to the barn!

An ambulance was waiting. The outside passenger even managed a little smile, even though he was hurting. The sergeant's name was Jim Kelly from Indianapolis. The man in the back was unconscious.

Before leaving the sergeant told me several soldiers were kept in a short, deep gorge a short distance from where I had first seen him. He and his friend had managed to slip up the side after dark and get away two days ago. He was concerned about the rest of those men, as they hadn't had any food or water for some time. Some of the men had been prisoners a couple weeks.

Later that day using the information from the sergeant, I flew over that area and on the third pass I spotted it. There didn't seem to be any sign of the Koreans so I flew low over the gorge. It appeared they were all dead, possibly in small groups with their hands tied behind their backs.

This information was then radioed back to headquarters.

I always wanted to be a fighter pilot. I did turn out to be a fighter. But now after seeing what I had seen, I was starting to think what I really wanted to do was get back and shoot some landings on the little grass strip next to the barn.

Perhaps, I would land on that dirt road by Beth's place and see if she would like to ride with me in that old Cub again. Dad would like that. Mom looking down would too.

~

10
Foolproof

Jim had been grouchy at Jenny this morning; she had jumped all over him again because he hadn't been out looking for work. Didn't she know he hadn't been feeling well? No, it wasn't because he had been drinking again. Sure, he had been out with the boys; you couldn't be stuck at home all the time. The girl, that just happened. She doesn't know about that so it couldn't hurt her. Driving around working off his frustrations, what was the matter with her anyway? He was getting damn tired of her riding him. He should just dump her. That started to go through his mind, something to think about.

Getting married eight years ago, everything had been going well, making good money as a real estate agent. Within a year Jenny had inherited half a million dollars from her grandmother. What was the best thing to do with the money? Security, looking to the future, they took out a million dollar life insurance policy on each of them.

Jim, being a realtor, located a beautiful home high in the hills a short distance from his work in Boulder. A hefty down payment, he was making good money at the time, monthly payments wouldn't be a problem.

They were living a little high, parties and the good things in life, but hell, wasn't that what money was for? A year ago they had bought matching cars, two Ford Escapes with everything, the works, all wheel drives and sun roofs. Proudly paying cash, his beautiful ruby red, hers an emerald green.

Would you believe within the month he was let go from work? They said it was because of the recession. He questioned it, knowing he had been missing some work, not having closed a deal in the last month. Well, they could just take it and shove it, there were other firms that would be looking to hire him. He had a buddy at a firm called WeGuarantee Realtors, having pushed a lot of business his way in the past.

His buddy, Gus, had always said, "You need a favor or a job, I'm always here."

Well, he had called Gus for over a week leaving messages. What was the matter with him? Jerking him off this way.

Finally after two trips, he caught Gus in, it didn't go well. Walking up, shaking hands, saying, "Hi, Buddy, how are you doing, got a minute?" Asked Jim.

Gus acted like he didn't know Jim.

"Geez, I'm sorry," said Gus. "I'm just out the door to meet a client. Call me tomorrow," and Gus started to walk away.

Going after him, Jim caught him by the doorway. Grabbing his shoulder saying, "Hey, I've done you lots of favors, made you a lot of money, you told me to look you up if I ever needed a job."

Gus said, "What are you talking about, you gave me a few cheap jobs you didn't want, and there wasn't enough money in it for you. Times are tough all over. Two of our agents were laid off this morning."

"You ungrateful scum, there are others who want me," replied Jim. Waking away, he heard Gus say, "I doubt it."

He was right, everywhere Jim went it was the same thing. A few said, "The word is out on you."

Now Jim knew he hadn't left on the best of terms. About this time he started thinking he could find other types of work but the only places that would look at him were the fast food places, only wanting to pay $7 an hour - he couldn't exist on that.

So, Jim started hanging around the house, living on unemployeement and a few beers which only made things worse. The wife was telling Jim to go back to school; her parents would help until he had something, perhaps something in the insurance field. The word insurance got to Jim; it wouldn't get out of his head. They could cash in their life insurance but that would only carry them a short time. Then, he thought, a million dollars could set him up for life.

"Now I love my wife but she had become a bitch," thought Jim to himself. "Could I do without her for a million bucks? You bet!"

Jim thought about divorce, but no, Jenny would get almost everything, he wouldn't get the million bucks, the house or the cars - she'd have to go.

Knowing he'd have to do some real hard thinking - it would have to be foolproof so he made a list of pros and cons:

1. Fall in the bath tub,
2. Use some car antifreeze,
3. Methanol (wood alcohol),
4. A fall down the stairs,
5. Hire someone,
6. Use a pillow,
7. Suicide,
8. Car accident,
9. House fire,
10. Insulin injection.

Looking over the list, No. 8 stood out. He wouldn't have to be present and the insurance would pay for the car. There was some kind of a catch in all of the rest - either he had to be present or a pathologist would be able to find trace amounts in the blood. The last few years the bathtub had sent many to prison.

Looking over No. 8, the car accident, he thought if her car went over one of the steep switch back, going down into town, the car would be totally demolished; it would land among the boulders. Nothing would be left except the money he would get for the car. It would have to be a closed casket funeral.

The problem, he knew nothing about the mechanical work-ings of cars. How could you make a brake fail on a curve? He knew she was a fast driver, she made him take a breath once in a while and he was known to push it.

The first thing he did was pick up a car manual for his type of car. Studying it, he was lost, not understanding any part of it. He was going to have to talk to someone that understood these systems.

In the meantime, he was going to smooth things over at home. No one could know they had been at each other's throats, because of his drinking and running. If he was going to do what he was planning, he would have to be above suspicions. He could do this, no doubt. Being a lot smarter, he was going to be the best husband, get on his knees if he had to, maybe some flowers along with an apology.

Stopping at a flower shop on the way home, it was a beautiful spray, the smile on her face; he was almost regretting what he was planning. By the end of the evening it was starting to work, always knowing he had a way with women.

Slipping away the next morning, driving, trying to get some ideas, he looked at several shops but nothing seemed promising.

A couple hours later, passing a car wash, there was a small sign on a building off to the side; it read "Fix-it-all cars." Next to it, a man sitting on a bench tipping a bottle. Driving into the carwash, washing the car and when no one could see, he reached down and let some air out of the right front tire and then the left rear tire.

Leaving the car wash, Jim drove to where the man was sitting next to the small shop - an empty bottle on the ground. Driving up, Jim said, "My instrument panel says I have something wrong with my tires, they're low on air or something, maybe it's the computer. Can you check it out; I don't know anything about cars."

Before Jim left the shop, Jake Tolbertt had replaced the TPMS (tire pressure monitor) in the right front tire, filled the left rear tire with air, saying, "Now as good as new," presenting Jim with a $150.00 bill.

Now Jim was no dummy, he knew if the stem had to be replaced, it was still under warranty, he could have taken it back to the dealership. Having found out what he wanted, Jim knew if a guy would cheat a person out of $150.00, with the right handling, he could be had.

The next day he was back starting to build a relationship with Jake. Standing, talking, taking a few drinks with him. Jake had his own story to tell and it helped. Jimmy just happened to have a bottle in his car to share.

Jake's business hadn't been good; he had lots of time on his hands.

One of the women he had been living with had no honor

about her. Can you believe he hadn't served half his six month sentence for bad checks, she had sold his car and left town. The one he was living with now was trying to sober him up - fat chance. She'd even set him up with an eye specialist. Hell, there was nothing wrong with him.

As they talked along the way, Jim learned Jake had been a mechanic most of his life in the army assigned to the motor pool. While in the Army, his first wife had left him. Getting out, he had worked with the Ford Motor Company a few years. Then, wanting to be on his own, he started his little shop.

Jim had been thinking, this might take a few weeks, gotta go slow. Feel Jake out and work into it. Friends were not made over night.

The more Jim was with Jake, the more he knew Jake was the man for the job. Beginning to tell Jake about his manipulative wife, how he caught her stepping a few times. Of course, they were all lies but you say what you have to. After one of these talks he said, "Sometimes I wish she would miss one of those steep curves and get me out of my misery." Jake saying, "You would be a hell of a lot better off."

Jim asked Jake if he knew how to fix the brake system so it would go out under heavy pressure on a curve. Jake said, "You would be surprised the way a car can be rigged," adding, "you should always have a back up to be sure."

They bantered over this for the next week. At this time, Jim was sure Jake would help him out. He could go ahead with the plan, they were buddies now. Jake said by the time the car finally landed at the bottom of the ravine, there would be no evidence left.

To help seal the deal, Jim slipped Jake a thousand dollars, promising after the accident as soon as the insurance company paid for the car, Jake would receive $5,000.00 cash, no paper trail.

Jim had made sure never to mention the million dollar life insurance policy on his wife or that he had to get a $1,000 loan from one of those loan sharks.

After the accident, he would cut ties with Jake, maybe do

some traveling to get out of the area.

The plan was foolproof, nothing could go wrong, he had every angle figured out.

Jim knew Jenny had a hair appointment with her hairdresser at 2 p.m., the next day and she was to visit her parents this evening.

She came into the house for some reason, her car wouldn't start. Telling her to take his ruby red this evening, he would call his friend Jake and have him over here early the next morning to fix her car. It would be ready for her hair appointment at 2 p.m.

After Jenny had left, he had contacted Jake to say the plan was on. He had disconnected the battery cable so her car wouldn't start. She had taken his car to see her parents. Telling Jake to be there early the next morning, he would have the garage all to himself.

Jenny, getting home that evening, was all smiles. She had been happy he had been so sweet, looking into the schooling, possibly as an insurance adjuster.

That evening, they made love, a going away present. That much he could do for her.

At 9 a.m., the next morning, Jake showed up as promised. It was no surprise he appeared to have had a few drinks.

Jim told Jake that both cars were in the garage, the keys are on the counsel, the garage door is open, go in and do whatever you have to do. No one will be out to bother you. I'll drop in to see you later on this afternoon. In about two hours, Jake could be seen driving off.

Jim wanted Jenny to be pushed for time so she would have to drive fast on the switch back curve to her hair appointment, so he hung around making small talk.

Finally he seemed to remember that he had to get going as he had an appointment at the school. Giving her a kiss, he was out the door; he wanted to be a long ways away when the accident happened.

He had driven a few miles and was approaching the switch back curves when the phone rang. It was Jenny.

"Do you know where Jake is, his girlfriend just called saying he was going to miss his appointment with his eye doctor," she said.

Jim asked, "Why does he have to see an eye doctor?"

"His girlfriend says he is color blind and is going to see if he can fix it," Jenny explained.

Just as Jim was speeding into the first switch back, Jenny added, "And my car still won't start."

The thought struck him: Color blind and the car won't start. Then he knew.

Taking his foot off the gas, it stayed down. Foot hard on the brake, it hit the floor, then he was flying off the road into space.

One of his last thoughts was, this won't be an open casket.

~

11
The Silver Star

The night had been a long one, they had come at us full strength, some making it through or over the concertina razor wire that helped protect our positions. Our guns were hot.

Thank the Lord for our little parachute friends shot high into the sky. They hung there with bright phosphorus light lighting up the whole area almost like day. We could see them coming, tangled and caught in the wire fences firing until the last was down. No more movement, no one could be alive out there. We were so tired. A new day, will have to get the men some sleep.

Looking down the hill behind us I could see him coming, a replacement I expect. My God, what are they sending us! Don't we have any full grown men left? And here is this kid trying to make the hill with a backpack bigger than he is, somehow he made it. Coming up to me, he saluted, "Sir, I have been assigned to your platoon." I could see his name was Dewey Danielson PFC (Private First Class).

I told him, "Dewey, you don't salute sergeants, you do not salute anyone up here. You will get someone killed."

He said, "Yes, Sir."

Looking at Dewey, there seemed to be something about him. I didn't know what. The older I get the harder it is to judge the age of these young kids.

Having him stow his gear, I took him around to the different gun inplacements introducing him to the other men from various states. Dewey was from Grand Rapids, Minnesota located in the northern part of the state and had been in the army only a short time. He seemed bright enough but seemed to hang back some-what. Perhaps it was because some of the men were World War II veterans, someone to look up to and respect.

Here it was a month gone, Dewey was carrying his load but you still thought he was too small and young. They should have kept him back in the states for more training and a chance to grow up.

The lieutenant had just told me I was to take 15 men out into no man's land on a patrol to see what was going on in a hilly sector to gather as much information as we could. If we got lucky and got a prisoner that would be alright but we're not to get into a fire fight as it would be hard in this hilly country to back us up. I was to take Dewey out with me. It was past noon when we started. Things were going well. I had our best man out front on point with Dewey to the rear protecting him as much as we could until he learned how we operated. Having been out about an hour going through a gulley with a very shallow creek between two large hills, the men were spread out around a hundred yards from the point man back to Dewey.

When they hit us, the point man went down with the first shot. The men took cover behind anything they could. The North Koreans had the perfect spot for an ambush. We were low, they had the tactical advantage of the high ground, high on the hill. We could not move an arm or a leg, if we did there would be a shot. One of the men started to move to a better position. A shot, he went down, hit in the leg.

I could see Dewey, he had found a good position way back where he was. He was not firing his gun, he was looking around. We were keeping them in check for now but it was going to be dark in a few hours. We knew what would happen then. With some help they would be all over us. Feeling sorry for the young kid, looking back to where he should have been, he was gone. For the life of me, I had not seen him move. Where could he be? I hoped he would get back to our lines.

Dewey had heard the first shot. Seeing the point man go down in the far end of the gully, he had gone to cover behind the boulder next to the little stream. He lay quietly some distance from the rest of the team. Not moving, his clothes blending into the rocks, he knew momentarily he was safe. Knowing the rest of the team was pinned down, what could he do? If he shot he would give his position away. Taking his time, he had been under pressure before and knew he needed a clear head. After thinking for a little while, he started to remove anything he would not need. Helmet and jacket were put behind a boulder, his canteen too. Taking his 30 caliber carbine, checking to see that the two banana clips were taped together, putting the rest of his ammo behind him, securing his knife.

In his mind he knew where the team was. He had the lay of the land firmly in mind. The general area of the North Koreans, they were on the high ground and would not move down until dark. Other troops would come with them. Dewey slowly moved an inch at a time slowly to the creek, sliding into the cold water. Could he do this? He had to or his team was dead.

Moving, just keep moving. It was summer but the water was cold. Shivering, he kept on moving a little at a time. Half an hour and he had gone a quarter of a mile. He could move faster now. He was making good time crawling in the little creek bed. Now moving up and out of the creek behind the rock, shivering, would he be able to shoot when the time came? He was cold to the bone.

He was now a half mile off to the side of the hill. Moving faster, he still had to do some stalking like he had in Minnesota while deer hunting. Time was passing, he had to be moving faster, he had to be in position soon. He could see movement in the distance on the side of the hill. He was even with the Koreans now but way off to the side.

Starting to feel warmer, climbing and moving, he climbed higher. He had to be at least a hundred yards higher than them if his plan was to work. He could see the two boulders high above the enemy, an ideal spot. He was almost there when he saw a movement. An officer, he thought laying there having a cigarette out of harms way. Relaxing, intent on what his men were doing below. One of his men was just laying there apparently wounded, unattended. While the officer thought himself quite safe lying between the two boulders, what to do? There was no firing going on, Dewey held the high ground. If he shot the officer, his men below would hear. He knew what he had to do. The officer was laying, his head down the hill and would not be able to get up and turn fast. Laying his carbine down, he took his knife from his scabbard. As quietly as he could in his wet clothes and boots, he went down and forward. Getting about eight feet from the man when he started to turn. Pushing himself as fast as he could, landing on the half turned man, knife jutting down and in under the jaw up to his brain. Holding him, he didn't make a sound.

Pulling the man up behind the rocks, he got his carbine. Taking his two grenades, putting them on the ground. Taking his time now, he located as many of them as he could. He would take the ones furthest up the hill first, waiting, a man in his sights, the firing started, he got the first one, then one more. Wait, the firing started, he got two more. They heard his last shot. Turning it on, he got two more. Throwing the hand grenades, that's all it took. They were running for the far ridge. Our team below saw them moving, getting one. The runners were soon over the ridge and going strong.

Working his way down the hill to the Korean's positions, he could see some hands in the air. There were three of them. Hands in the air, cross-legged, jabbering and no guns to be seen. The sergeant with his team below had no idea what was going on. Making sure it was safe to do so, an authoritative voice was heard saying, "Do not fire, we're coming down" and it was in English. Not believing what they were seeing, three North Koreans with their hands in the air with a wet, muddy, bloody kid with a carbine behind them.

The three searchers went up the hill finding eight bodies and the officer with a knife still in his throat. They took some important papers off him which were written in Korean. The interpreter went to the one Korean who was down, he was still alive. With some help, he might make it. Cutting his upper clothes off, putting sulpha in his wounds and dressing it the best he could. We did not have the time or the men to take him with us. He was somewhat lucid, saying something to the interpreter who then said, "We are going" as he headed down the hill at a fast pace.

Getting back to the sergeant, he told him what the wounded man had said to him. A regiment of North Koreans were due at any time for an attack on the American lines just after dark. The sergeant had the radioman working on the radio to get it fixed. The radio weighed 60 pounds carried on his back so he would be of no use carrying the wounded.

Some help could be gotten from the prisoners although they did not look in great shape. They were glad to be POW's. A man came running saying that troops could be seen coming in the distance moving fast. I had been keeping my eye on the kid; I had never paid that much attention to him before.

He was alert and sure footed.

We had to move. The kid had picked up one of the M1 rifles, heavier with a longer range than his small carbine. Also carrying many more clips of ammo, saying he would take his spot in the rear because he was used to it. He knew he would be doing rear guard action, putting a point man out front, we started back.

Going over this rough terrain and carrying wounded was going to be slow at best, not knowing if we would make it. The radio mike was still being worked on. Looking back, I could still see Dewey climbing the hill up to his two boulders and it was not to get the knife, I knew that.

We had been moving about 20 minutes when I heard the first shot in the distance. Measured, a few seconds apart, then a volley from a long distance. We were pushing it, carrying the wounded. It would still be an hour or more. Dewey had reached his two boulders high on the hill. Earlier it had been good for them, now it would be good for him. He waited, but not long, it had taken him 10 to 15 minutes to get to the perch. They were coming fast on foot probably having met up with the men that had fled earlier.

Some of them were coming quickly up the creek. It was not yet dark. Resting on the rock, sighting in 300 yards or more, three men came into his sights. He fired, one man grabbing himself went down. The other two kept on coming, he squeezed again. The side of a head seemed to fly apart. The other man went to earth. More of them were pouring through. Taking his time, some were going down but more were taking their place. They were shooting up the hillside now, not knowing where he was. Trying to stay low between the two boulders so that they would not see his muzzle flash. He was firing faster now, so many they were hard to miss. They slowed, not wanting to get between the hills. There could be shooters up both sides. They would not wait long. Already they were climbing both sides of the hill in a flanking motion.

Before coming up the hill, he had set two trip wires with grenades by the little creek. All these men coming would not see them. He would not go that way. Instead going down the far side of the hill into a valley to the top of the next hill. Setting up again waiting, he had been making good time not holding them back much. At this rate they would catch up to the wounded men before long.

The North Korean officers were well known for using suicide tactics with their own men to gain an objective. Now they were close to the end of the gorge and the little creek when their men hit the trip wires. They heard the spoon handles fly from the grenades. They knew. The grenades went off about the same time. Men were hit, some died. Others wounded dropped. They started pushing past the wounded. They were losing men. Coming out of the gorge the Koreans were hit by a hail of fire from the top of the next hill. Four men went down. Dewey was down to his last couple rounds.

The sergeant with the patrol could hear what was going on behind him. His radio operator had just informed him it was now working. They were coming out of the valley, the Koreans were entering from the other end. It didn't look like they were going to make it. He called headquarters asking for air support giving coordinates between the hills. They were just leaving and starting to fill with North Koreans. He requested a napalm drop into the valley behind him. It was their only hope. Knowing that Dewey was behind him and probably dead as he hadn't heard any shooting for some time.

It was only twenty minutes or so, they could hear those beautiful war birds coming. There were four of them coming in low, perhaps 1800 ft just over the hilltops. They seemed to be dropping napalm bombs in a pattern. (Napalm is a jelly like substance which is half jelly mixed with gas. When it hits it will leave a burning path 60 ft wide, the length of a football field, 50 ft high, nothing lives). There were at least two bombs for each plane.

The valley behind them was engulfed in flames. The sergeant looking ahead could see columns of men coming to help them. They would make it.

It was getting dark now. It looked to the sergeant that the only one lost this day was the one that got them out.

He could still see the kid coming up the hill that first day. Talk about someone misjudging someone. After getting the prisoners and papers to the headquarter units, his wounded taken care of, then going to see the lieutenant who sent them on the patrol that day, telling him about the kid and what he had done. Saving the team, putting the Koreans to flight, slowing down the pursuers and saving their lives again, saying he thought the kid was dead but at least he should be awarded the Silver Star. The lieutenant looked at him and said, "You really don't know who he is, do you? His name is Dewey Danielson. That you know but he was a Minnesota 145 pound state wrestling champ two years in a row. I don't think we will have trouble with a Silver Star, sergeant, but it is amazing what he did. He was here such a short time."

The sergeant headed back to his bunker. He stopped as he entered. A dirty, beat up kid was standing drinking a cup of coffee. He was at a loss for words. Finally he said, "How? I thought you were in the valley."

"Well," Dewey said, "I ran out of ammo on the hillside, not liking someone running up my backside, I decided to go over the hill and down the other side coming in just on the other side of you guys. Looking over into the valley I could see it was a might warm over there!"

"Think I'm a little tired. Got to turn in. Good night, Sarge."

He left me speechless again.

12
The Perfect Murder

The sign on the side of his real estate business said: Jim Dunstan, Realtor, White Bear Lake, Phone No. 612-218-0001.

Jim, sitting in his office the morning of August 1, 2007, thought he had it bad last night, didn't really know what the future had in store for him. He had walked into a restaurant with his employee and current girlfriend. Taking her light wrap, he hung it on the back of her chair and leaned over to show his love for her, squeezing her thigh with a light kiss on her lips. Looking up, he was looking into the eyes of his wife two tables away with three other women. If looks could kill. She never moved or got up. The other women could see what she was looking at, they understood.

Jim, thinking perhaps it would be best if he and his companion dined elsewhere, was soon hustling his bewildered companion out to the car.

Jim, before leaving home had been sure to give his wife a very detailed description of his heavy work load for the evening. Asking not to be disturbed as he would be working late.

He noted of late she had been asking some very pointed questions. In their 19 years of marriage she had never seemed to suspect anything when he would come home saying he would be out of town for a few days for a board meeting or a seminar. One time she said, "Maybe you would like me along for some company?" He had shot that down, saying, "You would be bored out of your mind and I would be worried about you and not get any work done."

Taking the girl back to where they had left her car, she was asking, "What is wrong?"

She didn't deserve an answer, if it wasn't for her, he wouldn't be in this trouble. The money that he had been spending on her that he didn't have. Dumping her off at her car, he just said, "Get out!" Leaving her standing there crying.

Starting to drive around thinking. His business was going under. The real estate business had practically no sales for the last two years helped in part by the fact he had not been paying attention to business. His other two salesmen had quit, going to work for other firms. Now all he had working for him was his secretary and leaving her the way he had, she may not be in tomorrow. His house had a high monthly payment, one he thought he could afford when the business was going well. Also, his car payment was overdue.

He didn't know what was wrong with that wife of his. Couldn't she see he was having money problems? After all, she was a nurse and could make big bucks. Sure, he had been in love with her when they were first married, telling her, "No wife of mine would have to work; the place for a woman was in the kitchen." Of course, that had changed after a couple years when Donna, the beautiful, the flirtatious secretary had gone to work for him. After that he was working many a late night to keep the business going, you know. Now he could lose everything, maybe cash in their life insurance policies but he didn't know how much that would bring in.

He had been driving around for some time now. Might as well drive home, face the old lady. He had put her in her place a couple times the last few years. He was the man of the house, she had always submitted to him.

Storming into the house, there she was watching TV. She didn't even turn to look at him. "Well, what have you got to say, lets get this over with." Very calmly she turned, looking him right in the eye saying, "I have known about all of your girls in the past. More so, I have called my attorney. We have a set appointment at 5:30 tomorrow in downtown Minneapolis on Chicago Ave. We will be there. You know where the guest room is, you will be sleeping there tonight. Also, you will pick me up at 4:00 tomorrow. There will be no discussions between us before we are at the attorney's office. Sleep well." She turned back to her TV.

She could not treat him this way. He started to say something, then thinking he would be better off without her. But, how did she know?

The next afternoon she had gotten into the car not saying anything. It was getting into the rush hour. He was speeding on I-35, might as well get this over with.

Getting close to the Mississippi River Bridge, now he was seeing break lights and a dust cloud in front of him, cars slamming into each other and skidding. What is going on? Looking across, you could see some of the bridge going down, cars going with it. Then he was stopping, his car half turned sideways leaning ready to go over. His door was easy to get open; the car was leaning that way. Getting out, he was able to get around the trunk of the car. Looking up the incline there were lots of cars. People running, screaming, no one paying attention to him.

There was a girl by a white van with her telephone probably calling her friends. The car was starting to slide slowly.

His wife could only get the car door open a foot or so and was part way out of it. If it went over, there was a 65 foot drop in this area. As he went to help her out, he thought about those life insurance policies. Someone was going to be sued over this mess.

She had her purse in her hand then it was violently pulled away. She felt the car sliding toward the edge 10 feet away, she might make it. Then she felt a fist hit her solidly in the jaw, then again. She was falling backwards with the car, smashing and rolling. Meanwhile, Jim was making it to the safe part of the bridge. Purse still in hand clutched to his chest, thinking she probably had a roll in there.

From what he could see, his car had landed in the water working it's way down stream, now only the top could be seen.

Soon police cars, fire trucks, and emergency personnel were appearing from all directions. As soon as he could he found a police officer, telling him what had happened. How he had tried desperately to get his wife's car door open, she had dropped her purse and went over the edge still trying to get out of the car.

As you looked over, you could see the main spans were down, 1900 feet of them, some falling over a hundred feet. The approach spans fell some 38 feet. The roadway itself made of reinforced concrete 27 inches in depth. You would not think anyone could live through that.

After finishing his report to the police, giving his car license and so forth, making sure they knew how he had fought to rescue his wife. He got a cab home. Knowing from what he had seen, she would not be found for some time.

Jim was quite elated when he got home. Thinking a million dollar life insurance policy on his wife would come in handy. Of course, when they found her, they would have a very expensive funeral for her. Maybe $8,000, no, $5,000 would be plenty. Everybody would be feeling sorry for him losing the love of his life. But now he had better call her parents, they could spread the news.

Jim received a call about 11:30 the next morning saying they had recovered his car with his wife in it. As it was a violent death, an autopsy would take place. He would have to come down to identify her. Jim was hardly listening to the police officer as he was so engrossed in what the man was saying on the TV. Already, they were asking for an investigation as over 10 persons were confirmed dead with many injured. The announcers were saying that some families could get millions.

Jim had dollar signs swimming in his head. The insurance company would be paying off his car and he would be collecting his wife's life insurance policy for a million dollars.

Talk about a perfect crime, he could not have planned this. He was even thinking how--- no he had to watch himself--- be careful what he says---think over what he had told them---remember every detail he had told them---write it down on a piece of paper and rehearse it. He was a lot smarter than they were, they had no reason to suspect him of anything. He was going to come out of this taken care of for the rest of his life.

The funeral had gone well; he had managed to save a few bucks. Also the donations from his rich relatives had been quite generous. But, of course, they should have been because they knew business had been bad.

Thinking back to her parents, they seemed much cooler the day of the funeral than the night he had called them about the accident.

It had been several months since the accident. The insurance company was getting ready to pay off. The charities and the state are being very helpful moneywise. Life was good.

This morning the police department had called asking if it would be convenient for him to come down to the station. They had a few minor details to clear up, and then they would be releasing their report to the life insurance company. Jim said he would be only too happy to assist them in any way he could. He would be there at the appointed time.

As Jim was entering the offices where he was to go over the details of the accident thought he recognized a young girl in the hallway, the one that had been calling her friends on the phone at the top of the cement when the bridge went down.

Entering the offices, he was met by a very charming detective, Sue Danielson. Shaking his hand saying, "Jim, I'm so glad you could make it, we have been so swamped as you know trying to put the finishing touches on everything." She led him into a side room where a Detective Hanson was sitting in a chair. Getting up, smiling, shaking his hand and thanking him for coming in on what must be a busy day.

Jim, looking around could see a lot of electronic equipment. Not knowing what it was, he felt a little uncomfortable,

Then the lady detective was saying, "Jim, what we are doing here today is that we would like you to describe everything you saw at the I-35 Bridge. People, cars, did you see any part of the bridge go down and if you did, what part of the bridge went down first? Then we want you to tell us personally what happened to you and then there will be a couple miner questions if you don't mind. This will all be video recorded and taped so we don't have to remember everything, do you understand what I have described to you?"

Jim saying, "Yes I do" but thinking, "Do you think I'm an idiot?" Also, he had rehearsed all his answers before coming down here.

Then she was saying, "Did you come down here today of your own free will, no one forced you or threatened you in any way? And you may leave at any time you wish. Do you understand that?"

Jim replied, "I understand."

Detective Danielson continued, "Fine, we will just get a few more things out of the way, such as name, date of birth, addresses and so forth. Please continue as this is all being recorded; please tell us about your day, about how you happened to be on I-35.

Jim started to tell how his day started having breakfast with his wife, kissing her goodbye and off to work. Doing a very good story, he thought of his day, there's no way they can check on this any way.

Then he was telling them how he was driving the speed limit otherwise he would have gone over the bridge, how he had heroically tried to save his wife. The officers seemed impressed at his bravery.

Having rehearsed his story given to the officer on the bridge that night, he knew they would not be able to pick it apart.

Then the officers were asking him a lot of irrelevant questions:

How long he had lived at that address?
 Five years.
Did he have a mortgage on his house?
Yes, $350,000.
Did he own his own car and was it paid for?"
Yes, but it's financed for $48,000.
Did he have life insurance on him and his wife, and if so, how much?
Yes, a million on both of them.
Had he up to this time filed a claim?
Yes, he had filed a claim on his wife's insurance for one million dollars.
Are there any clauses where the insurance wouldn't pay the amount?
Yes, if the person trying to collect would have murdered that person.
Had he received any compensation from the state?
Yes, he had.

"Jim, have you filed a lawsuit against anyone for your losses?" They asked. "If so, how much?"

"Yes, for $20 million for the loss of my wife," he replied.

He was starting to get a little uncomfortable.

"Jim, is it true you and your wife had an appointment with an attorney at 5:30 and if so, what for?"

This one floored him but he replied, "Just to go over business and finances."

Then, Sue, the detective said, "I think we have enough."

"Jim, I have a little video I'd like to show you, I think we have the motive, but I'm sure you would like to see this as you are going to be entitled to a copy anyway," said the detective.

At first the screen was showing a part of the bridge going down on the far side, some cars with it, then his golden Cadillac sliding part way over the edge and tilting like it might go over at any time and there he was working his way around the back of the car going to help his wife. The door partially open, heavy because the car was leaning to the far side almost ready to slide over the edge, you could see the leg and arm with the purse, she was almost out. The man approaching the car rips the purse from the women's hands. Then through the open window he is hitting the woman in the face with powerful strokes. She then falls back, leg outside the car; it is sliding over the edge and is gone. The man makes his way up the tilting concrete, the purse clutched to his chest.

Jim is dazed, thinking of the young girl talking to her friend on the phone. The detective is asking, "Are there any questions?" Then saying his wife had called her mother the night before and gave her a list of all his girlfriends and the reason they were going to see the attorney.

Detective Hanson was telling Jim to please put his hands behind his back as you are being charged with 1st degree murder. I will be putting the cuffs on you now. You will be booked into jail then if you wish you may have a phone call.

Jim was thinking, I was going to be taken care of for the rest of my life, but not this way.

~

13
The Locket and the Rose

Jerry was standing at the pier in Seattle, Washington waiting with hundreds of other soldiers to load onto the troop ship, *The General Howe*. Like everything in the army it was always hurry up and wait. Too much time to think, standing in line, always cold here on the coast.

How did I get here? He always knew he was to be a soldier. His mother, a beautiful woman never married, had told him when he was very young about his father. They had met while he was home on leave. She was at a dance for the boys that were going overseas.

There he was sitting by himself. She thought he looked so alone. Walking over she looked down into his eyes and felt dumbstruck. Such emotion. She started to feel weak in the knees, she had to sit down. Was she sick? She was only 17, what was happening to her? Then not looking at her, he took her hand and she saw a teardrop from his eye, like he had just been saved from some horrible fate.

After some time they got up, never saying a word, walked out into the night. This was their night, dark beautiful stars, a full moon just over treetops.

Walking to the river, looking down, they could hear the rushing water. Stopping, they turned to face each other, hands entwined. Breathlessly, they both waited. Then he said "My name is Gerald and tonight I found an angel." She then raised a golden locket that was around her neck. Looking closely he could see the name, Rose Marie, they both smiled.

He explained he had no one else in this world and had to report back in two weeks to be deployed on a special mission. He was never told what or where it would be but thinking it may have to do with China.

Looking at each other, they both knew what was about to happen. Coming close, that first touch, that magical moment, the kiss. They had to back off trying to breathe then they were close again.

It was late; he had better take her home. Her parents were up and were pleased to meet the young man in uniform.

They were both young spending every spare moment together. They were very much in love, expressing it in every possible way to each other.

Then the time was here, she was with him at the bus depot. Taking the golden locket with her name on it, she opened it to show her picture on one side and a yellow petal from a rose on the other.

Smiling, he took it placing it in his jacket over his heart saying, "Someday this will be yours again, "I promise."

The bus was leaving; they kissed, promising to write each other. She could see him looking out the back of the bus.

Every day there was a letter to each other, love and feelings flowed. A month later she wrote him saying she might be in a motherly way, worrying what his response would be.

It was immediate, a phone call, he was overjoyed! It was hard to make phone calls but the letters kept coming referring to their little one as "their Little Bear".

Then the last letter came with most of the words cut out, censored. He had been gone three months, she never heard from him again. Try as she might, all she ever got from the army was that he had gone overseas, then nothing.

Now it was time for Jerry to walk up the ramp onto the troop ship. He knew he was heading for Korea. Reading the papers he knew that on June 25, 1950, North Korea had stormed over the border into South Korea, overwhelming the south with over 90,000 troops, 150 tanks and a 100 fighter planes. They had driven almost to the end of the peninsula taking almost all of the south except a small 50x100 mile square area around Puson. The Americans had counter attacked landing in the middle of the country at Inchon and was starting to push the North Koreans back over the 38th parallel.

At this time the Americans had lost 6,000 men and the ROK or Republic Of Korea, 70,000 casualties.

The trip to Korea was not pleasant as the ship was battered by storms and 70 ft waves. Almost all of the thousand men on board were seasick, throwing up much of the time. The ship taking almost 18 days to make the crossing.

At last they were on Inchon Bay in Korea. Going over the side of the ship with full packs on their backs, climbing down 40 ft on rope ladders into the landing craft. The bay was somewhat secure but upon landing they were loaded onto the trucks and headed to where the fighting was taking place.

Soon after leaving Inchon, they were seeing burned out buildings, tanks and trucks with what others said were dead North Koreans in the ditches, most with poor equipment and tennis shoes on. This was getting well into September, Korea lies almost on the same parallel as Minnesota so the climate is somewhat the same with a lot of the large hills like Minnesota. As you get farther north it gets much colder as you get up into the mountains with roads in the valleys which our mechanized tanks, trucks and jeeps would be using. As we moved north we were oft times ambushed. Part of the time they would blow up the lead truck, blocking the road, then using machine guns and mortars to ambush us from the hillside. This was something they consistently did as we pushed further north into what was called the Chosin Reservoir a few miles from the Yula River. On the other side is China and it was down to 25 to 30 below zero.

On November 25, 1950, all hell broke loose. The first ROK troops were ambushed by the Chinese troops coming in the middle of the night blowing bugles and horns. They swallowed up some thousands of Korean troops. Then they were hitting the American troops and a lot of cases they were being mowed down by the hundreds sometimes stacked 6 bodies high in front of your machine guns but there were always more of them.

The Americans were now trying to pull back being overrun and slaughtered. At times being shot where they lay, the wounded and dead being stripped of their boots and watches.

Jerry had been in constant fire fights and up to a point thought they were winning but finding out the Chinese had their own tactics with the ambushes.

It was estimated there were 50,000 Chinese troops around us. What was left of Able Company tried retreating south.

The 1st, 2nd and 3rd Platoons were almost gone, over a hundred men. Many of the wounded left behind froze to death.

Jerry was up with his rifle squad trying to keep control of the bridge so the Regiment could retreat back south when they were hit with mortars and machine gun fire. The men were going down all around him. Then there was an explosion close by his side, he was flying off the side and lodged into a crevice. He blacked out. When he woke up he knew his left side was full of shrapnel, he was badly wounded. There was a body lying on top of him, trying to move, he had to get out of here. The body was just too heavy. A short time later he felt the body moving, but it couldn't be, the guy was dead. Then a voice saying, "Come on, son, let's get you out of there", and was being pulled up and out. Lying on the ground, he had been cramped up and cold so long he could not move.

Then he was on the man's shoulders being carried. Who was this guy? I weigh 150 pounds. Soon they were high in the rocks and it was morning. Lying there, he was feeling better but the blood had soaked his clothes and he couldn't stay warm. The man sitting close by seemed familiar but he couldn't place him. He was wearing sergeant's stripes.

Coming over, he removed Jerry's blood soaked jacket. Taking off his own jacket and putting it on Jerry that really helped a lot, but what would the sergeant do for warmth? Telling Jerry to stay behind the rocks, he would be back.

Within the hour he was back bundled in Chinese padded jackets with their earflap cap on. Going to Jerry he helped him put on a padded jacket and a floppy ear cap. Then he pulled out a bag of rice which didn't look to healthy but they ate some anyway.

That night, although he was in a lot of pain, they were working their way over the top of the mountainous terrain through rocks and snow. Very stealthy. One time coming to a large group of Chinese, 50 or more, someone said something to the sergeant and he roared back in what sounded like Russian and the man backed off.

The sergeant carried a pistol on his side, never taking it out. If we came to some North Koreans or Chinese he just acted like we owned the place. Walking through them like they had better get out of his way. We laid up sometimes in the daytime. This had been going on for five or six days.

The sergeant had dressed my wounds, some of them were deep. I was wearing down, getting weaker and slowing the sergeant who was always there to help me. He hardly ever spoke but sometimes I would see him looking my way but I'm not sure I was in any condition to listen. Sleeping, when we did stop, always cold. I don't know how many days we were out there. One morning we were back of some rocks by the road and here comes an American jeep heading south with several trucks loaded with wounded men. The sergeant removing his floppy hat stepped out and waved the convoy down.

Being loaded into the truck, I hadn't gotten the sergeant's name but I thought I heard him say, "See you, Little Bear" but I supposed I looked like that with my long earlaps and padded jacket.

We were taken to a field hospital, stitched up, then flown to a special hospital in Osak, Japan for treatment of frostbite of hands and feet. Then getting well enough being flown back to Persy Jones General Hospital in Battle Creek, Michigan.

After 6 weeks a medical discharge, I arrived home by bus. Greeted by a crying mother, saying I could not stand losing both of you.

A couple days later, I was emptying my duffle bag on the bed when Mother walked in and said, "Could you tell me how you were able to get out of North Korea?"

I looked at her thinking back on all the death I had seen, then trying to remember who had helped me, the sergeant. Telling her how the sergeant rescued me from the crevice, risking his life, carrying me on his shoulders until he was exhausted, helping me, directing us through the mountains, leaving out no detail.

How in the end I waved, "good bye" and he saluted me and hollered, "Good bye, Little Bear" and I probably looked that way with my Chinese jacket and floppy eared hat.

As I was telling her this, I was pulling the sergeant's jacket from the bag. I looked at her and she had the strangest look on her face, handing her the jacket which was dirty, bloody and needed a washing.

Taking the jacket from me, something fell out of the left breast pocket. She quickly picked it up and started to cry. Holding it in her hand, she showed it to me.

A golden locket with a name on it, Rose Marie.

Carefully she opened the locket, his mother on one side, a young man on the other. On the lower part of each picture, a part of a yellow rose petal. On the back of the locket, inscribed was:

Yours again, I promised.

Somehow Americans often forget what our troops sacrificed. In the Korean War alone, here are the statistics:
American troops: 33,000 killed; 105,000 wounded; 8,142 captured; 3,746 missing in action
South Korean troops: 415,000 killed; 429,000 wounded

~

14
The Pig Farm

Dan and Vic Swensen had lived on the old Swensen pig farm their entire lives, just a short distance from Remer or Shovel Lake on Highway 200.

The parents had always treated them cruelly making the boys work the farm, slopping the hogs, working the fields, cutting the winter wood with an axe and a saw. Most of the farming was done with horses; mowing, plowing and cultivating the corn.

The corn fields were many acres as the animals all had to be fed.

Vic looked down on his mother because she was obese, thinking she looked somewhat like the hogs he slopped every day.

The old man was small but strong, demanding respect, knowing how to use the old leather razor strap on their bare legs and sometimes elsewhere.

The only time the boys were getting off the farm was for school and a few times they were allowed to go to the cinema in Remer on a Saturday, perhaps a few times a year.

Vic was the bigger and stronger of the two boys, older by two years and very much the leader. Dan bowing to whatever Vic wanted. The boys hadn't done well in school, the 8th grade, their last year. There was work to be done.

The boys couldn't break free. The years were passing them by. They were growing resentful.

In 1947 both parents were drawing social security, putting some money in the bank. The boys were still under their thumb. The only time they felt free was when they would drive the truck with pigs or cattle to the South St. Paul stockyards, pocketing some of the money from the sale of the animals, having a good time before leaving town. They were getting older and the old man was loosing some control.

Then a tragic night for Dan, Vic took it as a blessing in disguise, the old man and the wife had been at the pub just outside Remer until closing time. Coming home in his nice shiny pickup, no one ever knew if he had tried to miss a deer or if it was the booze. He left the road, running into a large pine tree. The county sheriff thought they had died on impact, as the engine was driven back into the cab of the truck.

The boys made a decision to have both of them cremated; this would save money from having to buy caskets. The urns would be taken home. There would be no burial plots to take care of. Having a small funeral at a local church, the two boys, the minister and two elderly ladies from Shovel Lake attending.

It was back to the drudgery of farming, the boys acting like nothing had happened. Finding the books, going through them, they found they had several thousands in the bank.

As the Social Security checks came in, Vic would drive to the Deerwood bank some 70 miles away. Depositing them to their account, it was $1,200 a month for both checks. They were able to buy a new truck as the insurance from the wrecked truck covered the cost.

Money was starting to get a little low; they had been spending some time at the gambling casinos. Every couple weeks they were taking a load of pigs to the stockyards.

All the work was starting to get to them; they hadn't realized how much the old man had been doing. And the house, as big as it was with five bedrooms was starting to look like a disaster.

On a late spring day coming back from the stockyards they stopped at Rogers to gas the truck. Rogers is located on Highways 101 and 169 north of the Cities.

They struck up a conversation with an elderly hobo looking for a ride north, saying he didn't need much as he had Social Security and would be looking for some small jobs to get by.

This sounded interesting to Vic and Dan, as they were always in a hurry to get back, the animals had to be taken care of.

Telling Mike, the hobo, they had extra bedrooms at their place, he could do chores and have a place to stay. He would have plenty of time to think it over on the way north. They also had a junker of a car if anyone wanted to run into Hill City or Remer.

On the drive back, Dan could see Mike was wearing a Mickey Mouse wrist watch, thinking that was strange but he said nothing.

Arriving at the farm, Mike could see there was going to be lots of fixing up around the place. His room had not been used for some time, was cleaner than the rest of the house. Going to bed early, turning off his gas lantern, the farm had no electricity. His arthritis was starting to act up but at 75, who could complain?

At first light he was out fixing a gate then walking around to get a lay of the place. It didn't take long to see that it had possibilities. This was a good piece of land with a couple of good barns and plenty of sheds for the 80 or so hogs. He had seen four cows and four horses that seemed to be good stock. A few chickens were in the yard scratching about.

Mike got along with Dan, shying away from Vic, who always seemed ready to explode, doing so over little or nothing. As the days wore on he came to enjoy his work, always busy. Shortly after arriving he had sent a letter for a change of address. Within two weeks his first Social Security check arrived in the mailbox. Vic, hadn't realized it wasn't his mail when the check came and had mistakenly opened the envelope, seeing it was for $730. Saying he was sorry, Vic handed it to Mike.

Vic, while getting the mail was very curious as to what Mike's check would be, pretending he had opened it by mistake was quite surprised at the amount. This started his mind rolling, with another $700 added to the parent's checks they could be doing very well.

Mike had learned quickly, some of the pigs could be very dangerous, so if he was among them for some reason, he carried an axe handle. It was always the boars you had to watch out for.

One day a small sow got caught up in the barbwire, getting loose, bleeding down the length of her side. She was walking through the deep mud when a boar knocked her down, then the squeals began. In 15 to 20 minutes all that was left was a few bones and blood and they were trying to eat those bones too.

Mike thought, "If I hadn't seen this, I wouldn't have believed it." From then on, his axe handle was always with him.

In the middle of the summer, Vic started to send Dan to the stockyards saying he could handle it. There was just too much work on the farm for the both of them to be gone. Mike and Dan were putting up hay and working the cornfield, it was getting into September when Mike mentioned he could be heading out one of these days, it was time to be heading south.

The next day Dan headed for the stockyards with a load of hogs. Thinking they were doing pretty good he decided to hit a few beer joints and stay over night. Driving into the farm after 6:00 the next evening, his head still pounding from the night before and a few he had while driving home. Driving into the yard, he didn't see Mike. Vic was filling a hole just inside of the pigpen. He saw Vic hit a pig that came too close, and then he was in the house getting something to eat. By this time, the way he felt, he was going to bed.

Dan never heard his brother or Mike go to their rooms. He was the first one up the next morning, to his surprise, because almost every morning Mike had been up, coffee made and out the door.

In a short time Vic came down the stairs looking and acting surely, not saying anything, getting a cup of coffee, setting down. Dan finally said, "Where's Mike, is he sick, generally he's down by this time?" Vic sat for a few minutes finally saying, "He left, he's gone, good riddance. We had an argument over how much I owed him for his work around here, I gave him $200, he took a few of his things and left. The last I saw he was walking toward 200."

Dan sat there thinking, "Something's wrong, why would he leave with his favorite coat behind the door?" Starting to say something, the look on his brother's face said, "Challenge me!" Thinking, "Get out by yourself, do your chores and do some thinking." From that day he knew there was something wrong with his brother.

Time for the mail, Vic would say, "I'll get it." Coming back one day with all three Social Security checks, that afternoon he drove to Deerwood depositing the checks to their account, stopping in Aitkin with some identification to cash Mike's check.

The week went by pretty tense and then Vic said he would be taking the next load to the stockyards. The next morning after loading the truck, he said "I could be late coming back."

Dan was doing his chores, something was bothering him. After an hour he could take it no longer. Going to Mike's room, which he had not entered since Mike had left. Most of his things were thrown into a corner along with some boots. Those had been the boots that Mike had on when he arrived and the only pair he had. Leaving the room as he found it, going outside, picking up a shovel, he made a guess where he had seen his brother filling a hole a couple weeks ago. Driving some pigs away, hitting them with a shovel. He started to dig about a foot and a half down, there was something. Reaching down he pulled Mike's shirt from the muddy hole. Something else was down there, pants and shorts. There should be a body, where was it? Looking over about 8 ft in the mud, he saw something white. Walking over and reaching down, he pulled out a small bone. Next to it was a black band, wiping it across his pants; it was a Mickey Mouse watch. He knew then where the body was.

Hurriedly, he put the clothing back in the hole, covering it with dirt. Then driving several hogs over it covering his tracks, Dan cleaned the shovel off and put it back. He started to sweat but tried not to think his brother would do anything to him, yet he kept coming back to that challenging look he had received from his brother and felt tightness in the back of his neck.

About 11 a.m., Dan could see a large black car making its way up the driveway. Two men stepped from it. They looked like money. Approaching him they handed him their business cards, introducing themselves as cattle buyers. They were looking for a farm to buy in this area as they would be buying a lot of cattle and would need a place to hold them while making arrangement to send them to market. Asking would he be willing to sell the farm at a reasonable price. Dan thought about it, thinking it would be a good time. He knew Vic would not go for it. Still, he asked them how much they would offer. Knowing they were way out in the sticks, they were thinking in the area of $25,000, $20,000 was for the land and $5,000 for the livestock. Dan knew land wasn't going for much in the early 50's, but they should be getting twice that amount. He told them, no, not at this time but he would be talking to his brother. The buyers left saying they had other places in mind but he had a month.

Vic didn't make it home that day, arriving the next day in the late afternoon with a guest, as he put it, a man about 45 years of age with a noticeable limp. Sticking out his hand, the man introduced himself as Kennedy White, "Just call me, Ken," he said. Vic explained he had met Ken in a bar; they had had a few drinks together, finding he had been wounded in the Korean War and was drawing a small pension. No relative, just looking for a place to lie down for a short time. Having gotten along so well, Vic had invited him to do light chores and to keep an eye on the place if they had to be gone.

One thing you could say about Ken, he may limp but he was as strong as an ox, being a welcome addition as he enjoyed farm work since he had been raised on a farm near Worthington.

Dan's mind was again bothering him; he had learned Ken had a veteran's pension coming each month. Two weeks later a check arrived. Vic had gotten the mail that day, had mistakenly opened it, seeing the check was for almost $1500. Vic had apologized for having opened his mail. Ken saying it could have happened to anyone.

The next few weeks, Vic was always with Ken working together. He never seemed to get mad like he used to, building up a trusting relationship. The closer they got, the more Dan thought about what had happened to Mike, the hobo. He couldn't go to the sheriff, who would believe him? There was no body, knowing by this time what would happen to him if his brother knew what he was thinking. He shuddered at the thought of being thrown to the pigs.

What could he do? If he said anything to Ken who might think he is kidding, he could say something to Vic.

One evening just before dark something happened to the windmill. As it was pumping water for the animals it broke down. They would have to wait until morning to fix it.

The windmill was 40 feet tall with a small 2 foot wide platform built around it to work on the top. On the side was a metal ladder to climb to the platform.

As Dan came down for coffee the next morning, Vic told him he could go about slopping the hogs and the morning chores. He and Ken would be climbing the windmill to fix a couple loose blades and whatever was jamming the gears.

Dan started to say something, and then stopped, seeing the look on Vic's face, starting to feel sick inside. He had never challenged Vic and the fear rose up inside him. He turned, walking out the door. The tears started to come. Ken by this time was starting to feel like a brother more than Vic, yet he felt helpless.

Dan had never come close to saying a prayer in his life. As he went about his chores, he kept saying, "God, help me, God help me." Realizing he didn't even know how to say a prayer. As he worked, he always had an eye on the windmill. Soon, he could see the two blades had been repaired. The two men were working on the gears, neither one of them had a safety rope tied to them, always moving cautiously.

Dan was watching, and then he KNEW. Ken was bending over to pick up a tool. Ken hearing Dan holler, grabbed a cross rail looking down at Dan. Just as Vic stumbled into him, Ken never knew what happened. As he started to fall he hung onto the bar and was hanging onto the side of the windmill. Vic, losing his balance, reaching out, falling as he went by Ken, grabbing for something and then he was gone.

Dan watched his brother falling, landing half out of the water tank over a sharp edge realized he was still saying, "God help me, God help me." Looking up he could see Ken had climbed around to the ladder and was coming down the side of the tower. Running over, there was nothing he could do. As Ken came over, Dan said, "I saw it all." Vic lost his balance almost taking you with him, it was an accident."

Ken took the truck to a farm close by to call for the sheriff who took a good half hour to arrive. Then an ambulance arrived, there was some questioning, some paper work. The body was placed in the ambulance, leaving without the lights on.

The two men stood and talked for some time. Dan again said how he had seen Vic lose his balance almost taking Ken with him. Ken saying how sorry he was for Dan, losing such a wonderful brother.

They walked back to the house together. Dan, thinking, I haven't breathed this easy in a long time.

It seemed the next few days flew by, chores to be done, a small service like the one for the parents. Vic had been cremated. Dan, Ken, the minister and the two ladies from Shovel Lake attending.

The next day Dan had gone to Grand Rapids, called the cattle buyers. Yes, they were interested at their price. He accepted, they were to take over in one week, the end of the month.

Contacting Social Security, telling them the parents had died, also that Mike had moved on leaving no forwarding address.

He had signed the old car over to Ken saying he had no further use for it, they parted as friends.

Knowing when he had hollered at Ken at the top of the windmill, he had somehow saved his life. But, the words inside of himself, "God help me, God help me," had somehow set him free for

111

the first time in his life.

Now was his day, a Sunday, he would be leaving here forever, he knew what he would be doing, driving the pickup to the little church in Hill City, then leaving to a freedom he had never known.

There was one last thing he must do, going to the mantle in the living room, he took all three urns, walking over the land he spread their ashes, this was their home.

~

15
Lonesome Girl

My name is Heather, I am 13 years old. Mom gone, Dad is a great guy but living in a daze on a farm 20 miles from nowhere. A big silo, big barn and some out buildings, a two story house with covered porches on both sides on 160 acres with no crops, just big hayfields.

My dad, Jim, is gone a lot, he works for neighboring farms as a handy man. Sometimes it seems the only things I see are a few deer in the fields and flocks of pigeons flying around the silo and barns.

The few chores I have don't take very long and you get tired of radio and TV pretty fast. The summers are long so I start to look forward to school.

The one thing I truly enjoy is riding with my Dad when he has time on our twin 1984 200S Honda three-wheelers. When he is not here I'm restricted to riding on our hayfield, but when we're together we take a lot of back trails, sometimes for miles.

This morning it had been raining. The sky is starting to clear and a warm beautiful sun is starting to shine. I'm thinking of taking a ride.

Walking by the barn to get to the shed where the Honda's are, I see something moving in the muddy road. At first I can't make out what it is. It's all wet, looking like it had been there a day or two, it seems almost lifeless. Picking it up, it is some kind of a bird maybe a week old with wet feathery down sticking to its body.

Looking up, I see pigeons flying and moving around but I have no idea where this one came from. Not knowing what to do, I thought I would take it back to the house. Maybe clean it up, get it warm, then think of what to do next.

Getting back to the kitchen, I got a bowl out of the cupboard and put some warm water in it. Putting the baby bird part way in, I washed the dirt and grime from it, then patted it with a dry fluffy towel until its down seemed quite dry. During this time it just sat there not appearing too strong but opening its little beak once in a while.

If it had been there a day or two, it could not have been fed. Now what to do? Thinking it was cold, I wrapped it in a terry cloth towel next to a 100 watt lamp bulb.

It was too young for hard food. Going to the cupboard taking some oatmeal down, I soon had some warm mushy oatmeal ready. Getting a large eyedropper, I squeezed some into its mouth. It seemed like some of it was going down. I thought not too much at first, there would be more feedings, then every couple hours until Dad got home at 6:00 tonight.

When he got home, he looked all tired out. After helping him get something to eat, I told him I had something to show him. I took him to the porch showing him what I had wrapped in a towel still by the light bulb. He looked at the little thing and said, "That's a baby pigeon. Where did you get it?" I told him how I found it and about the cleaning and feeding. He seemed surprised but said he didn't think it would make it.

He then told me that many years ago before I was even around, he had kept a loft of many pigeons. There were three groups, fancy, racing and utility pigeons. Squabbling, the latter, were for eating. But the fancy were for tumbling, high flying and were fun to watch doing all kinds of acrobatics in the air. The ones he had raised were racing pigeons. Some can fly from 50 to 110 mph for long distances up to 1,100 miles.

Dad told me, if this one made it, we would be able to know what kind it was by looking into its eyes. If there was a dark pupil with red to yellow coloring around it and the eyes were not dry, we had a quality racing pigeon.

Feeding it once more before going to bed, I said a little prayer.

Getting up early the next morning, I warmed up some oatmeal. As I approached, the mouth came open and the head came up. I'm thinking, "He's going to make it."

By the end of the day on Sunday, I knew for sure and I knew that his name was to be, Sunny, for he was bringing joy to my heart. So needy.

Now I was keeping him in a large bird cage, feeding him pellets that Dad had brought and reading the book Dad surprised me with on feeding and raising pigeons.

As time was passing, the bird was developing a beautiful dark green head. Dad thought it was a barred starling. It's tail was as dark as the head. After examining it's eyes he said, "You have a high quality bird there."

Then Dad laid out a small loft for me to build with his help on the porch outside my upstairs bedroom.

Having hand fed him for so long, he had trust in me. Also, I could whistle quite well and as I went about he would follow me landing on my shoulder as I walked.

I started to take him on my three-wheeler very slow at first then a little faster although Dad had put a governor on the machine saying a three-wheeler was very dangerous. Every time I went for a ride I was to leave a note.

Many a time, I would look and Sunny would be way up in the sky. If I would whistle loudly he would sweep down to me.

Knowing Dad was being good to me and trying to protect me by restricting me to the pastures when he was not home, I was starting to push it going on a few close trails then a little further. I know it was wrong but he didn't know.

Sunny seemed to be everywhere, then gone. Sometimes I wouldn't see him again until I got back to the loft. Then I started to go further up past the monster rock with the soft sand. Dad and I had ridden it many times before.

I was taking Sunny further and further each day to have some fun. Whistling to Sunny, I would attach a note to his leg and send him off. The note was to me but when I got back there would be Sunny in the loft with my note. I was telling Dad how well he was doing, not telling him how far I had gone.

One day, a Saturday, Dad would be working until noon. At 1:00 he would pick me up, we were going to go shopping for school clothes. Thinking I had time for a little ride, going to my Honda, I pulled on the rope. No matter what I did, it would not start. I was in somewhat of a hurry so had not taken the time to let Sunny out of his loft. I thought I would take Dad's three-wheeler. I had been told not to take it but I would be back early, no one would know.

Going out to the field was great, then thinking what the heck, got a lot of time. Coming to the monster boulder, going around in the soft sand, there was a small wash out. Thinking quickly, I squeezed the throttle. Forgetting I was on Dad's machine, it lunged and I was rolling in the sand. My right leg was in pain. I couldn't move it. The machine was almost on top of me.

That's when I remembered I hadn't left a note nor had I stayed in the pasture. Dad wouldn't be home for an hour.

Jim drove into the yard at 12:45, expecting to find Heather ready and waiting. Going into the house, calling her name, nothing. Stepping outside, calling her name, nothing. Checking the table for a note, nothing. Looking, he could see the bird in the loft. Then walking to the shed, he could see his machine was gone. Wondering why she had taken his, he tried her machine. It wouldn't start. A fast check showed the spark plug wire was broken next to the plug.

Quickly repairing it, he was soon over the fields, she should have been there. He had no idea where to look and it was getting close to 2:30. He was concerned. This was not like Heather, she was so dependable.

Riding back to the house, looking up, an idea came to him. Going to the loft he knew they had been inseparable. He took a small piece of paper and small pencil tying them both to the bird's legs. Taking Sunny outside, lifting him into the air, up he went in circles high then turning, he flew toward the pastures. Circling then he flew very high up over the trails disappearing in the distance.

Heather had been laying there a good two hours. Not hearing anything, hurting. She should have Sunny with her. She knew she had been so wrong. She knew Dad would be out of his mind not knowing what to do.

Did she see something high in the air? No, it could not be, she had left him in his loft. Dipping and diving like he flies. She tried to whistle, then louder. A couple more times, the spot was coming down straight as an arrow finally landing on the handle bars a few feet away. He had something on his legs, paper and a small pencil.

She started to whistle very softly. Holding out her hand, Sunny hopped to her hand. She stroked the bird, talking to him then removing the paper and pencil. Never letting go of her friend, she drew a squiggly line on the paper with a monster rock and a X on the bottom. Fixing it to Sunny's leg, she tossed him into the air. He flew to the handle bars and sat there looking at her cocking his head, then he was climbing high circling, disappearing.

Jim had been waiting, hoping. A half hour went by then almost an hour. There he was, flying to his loft. Jim walked quietly up the stairs. The pencil was gone, not the paper. Closing the outside door to the loft, he slowly approached the pigeon as he softly talked to him.

Reaching out, he lifted him very carefully, removing the paper gently and setting him down. Unfurling the paper, he expected words. What was he seeing? Turning the paper over, seeing the X, looking further he knew it was the huge rock.

She could hear him coming; she could see the pigeon high in the air. Her father was sliding down the sand, water, bed sheet and rope in hand.

Standing there looking, he started to cry, she held him. As soon as he could, he said, "I was so worried." And she replied, "Forgive me, Dad" as they had their arms around each other.

He was checking her leg. A bad sprain. Folding the sheet over and wrapping it around the knee, then using the rope he was able to stabilize it. Lifting her carefully, he put her on the running machine. Tying her leg into place, they now got on the lower trail. Then getting his Honda, he came to meet her. Using her good leg, she could brake with it.

It was getting dark when they got home. She thought she was going to be all right. As he was putting her to bed, she could hear the cooing from the loft.

The last thing she heard him say was, "As a little reward, I think we are going to have to get a mate for your friend."

~

16
The Hobo and the Dog

Here I am, Jim Bold, 10 years in the service and I'm out on my ear. Get out or get Court Marshaled supposedly for hitting the lieutenant in a drunken brawl and I don't hardly touch the stuff.

My attitude hasn't gotten any better after that. Call me a drifter, hobo or whatever. Family all gone, girlfriend married my best friend. What's left, take it and stuff it.

Spent the last eight months in Minneapolis, don't know why I came here. I think it is colder than Alaska.

This summer has really been hot. I think I'll go down to the Burger King and dumpster dive. Gotta eat, you know, then find a grate or a doorway for the night.

You always have to be careful walking the alleys in the southwest part of town. There is a mix of every kind so before I walk on, I stand and study it for some time. It's not too bad this late in the day but I have a set of brass knuckles in my pocket and a short knife to stay legal, you know.

About half way down the alley, I hear something, almost like it is in pain. Looking over the fence I could see a burned out car with trash all over the yard. In the middle of the yard is what looks like a skeleton of a dog, maybe a German Sheppard on a 10-foot chain. No water or food and it doesn't look like he's had any for some time. Fairly young, beat up and filthy. What kind of people are they? Well, it's none of my business. Looking at the dog, it raises its head. Looking at me, I hear a low whine, then it drops its head.

Like I said, it's none of my business. Looking around, I head for the Burger King dumpster a half a mile away. You really can't believe what people throw away, some of it untouched. This night is a smorgasbord. Eating three nice burgers, I still have four nice ones left. Putting them in a sack along with two bottles of water, then of course, I had to think of that damn dog. What the hell, I have to go back that way.

It's getting dark now, the street lights are coming on. I don't owe anyone anything.

Stopping at the end of the alley, then standing watching. Fifteen minutes go by. A light goes on in the front of the house. Taking my time, I move slowly down the side of the alley. Looking over the fence, the dog lifts his head. Now, what? I can't throw a burger that far to the dog. Standing there thinking, oh, crap, you can get killed like this.

Slowly, I opened the gate, it squeaks. I drop down, the dog doesn't move. I wait, moving slowly to the dog. Taking a hamburger, I try to give it to him. He won't take it. Looking, I realize the collar is too tight. The dog can hardly breathe or swallow. Checking the house, nothing moving there. Very slowly, reaching down trying to unbuckle the collar and finally it drops off.

The dog had gotten to its feet a little unsteady. Saying, "Come on, boy," he followed me to the gate. Now what the hell am I doing? I have no place for the dog and it's not my dog. Thinking there were some abandoned buildings four to five blocks away there was a small shed that might work.

I tell you, this was no greyhound as I had to keep waiting for him to catch up. Getting to the shed and forcing the shed door open, I pushed the dog inside. For some reason, he did not like it there. Taking the burger out, placing it on the floor, he wouldn't eat it. Remembering a rusty old pan outside, I got it and poured the water from my bottles and sat it in front of him. He looked at it for a moment, then started lapping until it was gone. Walking over to the burgers, he ate one and then walking to a corner he laid down. Thinking about where I had left my coat and bundle, leaving the dog, I was back in a half hour. Might as well spend the night just to see how he would do.

The next morning a couple of the burgers are gone, he looks a little stronger so I take him out so we can take care of our morning business. Putting him back in the shed, walking over to a small park, spending most of the day there walking by the creek.

Walking by a car wash on the way back to the shed, there was an old man trying to lift two truck tires into a pickup so I helped him out. As I was walking away, he said, "If my kids were any damn good, they would be doing this, they want everything for nothing. They're step-sons, the hell with them."

Getting back to the shed, the dog was happy to see me and

seemed a little stronger. Taking him out to do his business, I noted that the other burger was gone. I had filled up the bottles from the creek and poured them into the pan.

Putting the dog back in the shed, I started for the Burger King not going the way of the alley but by the car wash. The old man was working late.

Getting to the dumpster, I did very well. Heading back to the shed, the old man was still there.

After a couple days it was time to take the dog with him, not going down the alley but around by the car wash. The old man always seemed to be there. This went on for a week. The dog was starting to fill out, looking much better. As we went by this time the old man said, "Your little friend there sure could use a good wash job. If you would like to bring him in, I'll help you soap him down." The dog stood surprisingly good as they tried to work the matted fur out. He was starting to look like a new dog. In fact, a beautiful dog with silver tipped ears and muzzle. All cleaned and dry, he looked like a show dog.

As the old man was talking, he said, "I don't want to burden you but I sure could use a little help around here. There is a pretty nice room in the corner, room enough for both you and the dog. Think about it, I'll pay you a fair wage." I told him, "Let me sleep on it, I'll talk to you tomorrow."

The shed was not the most comfortable place to sleep. To hell with it, I wasn't mad at the old man.

Early the next morning I took Silver Tip with me to the car wash. The old man was there working already. I asked, "When do you want me to start?" He said, "You're here, let me show you around," handing me a set of keys. The morning was spent walking around, learning what had to be done and how to do it.

Surprisingly, I took to the work and was enjoying it. The old man gave me the key to all the vending machines telling me to take what I needed.

The two step-sons had been coming around. They seemed not too happy seeing me working there, saying if I stayed too long, it might not be good for my health. But, still they would not offer to do any work.

A month went by and one day the old man said, "Drop into the office, I would like to talk to you."

The old man said, "Jim, you are really a good worker, I like your work ethic. Here is what I am proposing to you. I would like you as a partner. I'm just getting too old to run the place by myself any more. I would set it up so that you would own the place in five years and I will retire, what do you think?"

I thought for a moment and told him it was surely tempting but "I wouldn't want to take advantage of you and what about the boys?"

The old man responded to that rather strongly saying, "Their mother took off five years ago and they have just been living off me ever since. They're in their late twenties and its time they were out on their own."

We shook on the deal, the old man saying he would be giving the boys the good news.

About 1:00 in the morning, I was awakened by Silver Tip. There was a lot of noise by the door; someone was trying to get in. Stepping to the door, I put my brass knuckles on. As I opened the door one of the boys swung a bat hitting the top of the door frame. Before he could swing again, he had a face full of brass knuckles, some loose teeth, a face full of blood and was falling down. The other boy had a knife in his hand, stepping back and the dog was on him. Turning to run, he slashed the dog's shoulder. The boy was running trying to dislodge Silver Tip who had a good grip on his rear.

As I looked down at the fallen boy, I told him I would be calling the police in a half hour and that they would be getting 20 years apiece for attempted murder. The boy went out the other door as the dog was coming back in through the other.

A short time later the old man showed up asking what was going on, saying the boys had come home beat up and in a hurry to leave. One of the boy's pants was ripped and bleeding from the rear also appearing to be in pain.

After I told him what had happened, I explained that Silver Tip would have to be taken to the vet as he had a deep wound in his shoulder.

Arriving at the vet, Silver Tip was taken care of soon. When the vet asked where I had found what appeared to be a very valuable dog, I told him. The vet said he would check to see if he had been micro chipped. Spending some time investigating, he got an answer. He said the dog's name was, Silver Tip, "the same name you gave him!" The dog was stolen some 8 months ago in Denver, Colorado while being presented at a dog show.

"The owners will be notified, you can work it out with them," the vet told me.

A few days later a very nice car pulled up to the side of the car wash. A young couple got out of the car along with a teen age boy on crutches. I looked down at Silver Tip. He immediately went on the alert and his tail wagged just once, then he stood still. The boy's mouth dropped open and he was on the ground with the dog all over him. The father said, "I don't know what to say."

"It's been said," I replied, looking at the two of them on the ground. Silver Tip belongs to the boy.

That's when I learned, by helping others, you sometimes help yourself.

~

17
The Three-legged Fox

Being a young farmer isn't always easy. Some years ago I inherited a small farm way out in the sticks. For some time I didn't know it was for me. Just finishing a stint in the service, parents were gone but 80 acres out in the pines sure looked good. Small barn and a big chicken coop next to a lake, just getting by, didn't need much. Having been saving my pay, had a nice little nest egg. A play on words since I was raising chickens, selling the eggs and a little fishing besides.

Come spring letting the chickens out, they were covering some ground, come time to roost they would go to the coop. The ones that were laying were kept penned in next to their coop.

Having a lot of chickens, it's pretty hard to keep track of them. Walking down by the lake one day I could see a lot of feathers and that was about all. Looking around I was able to find a footprint in some mud, it looked like a fox to me. As old as the feathers had been it must have been at least a week or so. Probably just one passing through.

Nothing happened for at least a week and a half when I stumbled upon more feathers in the woods a ways. Now I knew I had a problem. One evening sitting in my chair, looking down by the lake there was some movement. Couldn't make it out for a minute. It was my fox, beautiful red of summer.

This was my chance. Very quietly getting into the shack, picking up my 3.06 rifle with my sling on it, getting back to the porch, I raised that puppy up sighting in between two bushes waiting for Old Red to come into view. There he is, mine, no way I can miss. What's a hundred yards? Pulling the trigger, "bang," nice recoil. Cheek firm on the stalk, ready for another shot.

That fox must have gone two feet in the air and was gone, no way could I miss, but I did! Must have laughed myself sick for a couple minutes seeing that critter jump that high.

That sure didn't stop him, the next day I found more feathers. Starting to think I was losing a chicken a week.

Thinking there was more ways to skin a cat; I got some of my traps out and set four of them, being careful as the chickens could step in them. Baiting them with some gizzards, checking the traps every day, I was surprised to find a chicken had been caught in one of them. The other surprise was that most of the chicken was gone. Here I am trapping the chicken for the fox. A few days later I found a dead chicken in another trap. Thinking this may be the answer, I got a trap and set it under some leaves next to the dead chicken.

The following day going back to the chicken, part of it was gone. There was something in the other trap. There had been a lot of action there. You could see at least four inches of a fox's foot and leg in the trap. Now I've heard of this before but never believed it, but here was proof.

What I thought of that fox shot sky-high and the more I felt like crap setting that trap. Well, that was the last I'll see of him.

Taking my canoe fishing the next week, casting the shoreline I popped a few bass close to the shore.

We'd had a big blow some time ago, what a mess had been made of those big pines. Lots of them down with roots out of the ground.

Getting down shore about four hundred yards from my shack, I saw some movement, not making out what it was right away. A kit or baby fox next to a burrow under the roots of a tall pine tree and the mother limping close by. Now I really felt like crap!

I thought for a few minutes getting close to the shore some 200 feet from the burrow, I threw three bass up on the shore. If she couldn't catch anything maybe these would help.

Getting back to the shack, I must be coming down with something tossing and turning all night.

Well, if you can't sleep it must be you aren't working hard enough and there was a lot to be done so I threw myself into it. Three or four days went by; I really knew it was the bitch and the kit. What to do? I knew she liked chicken so I caught a couple of them and was soon on foot heading for the burrow. I would just leave them close.

It was a nice warm day, the only thing was there were lots of pine down, climbing down and through them was slow going.

Jumping down from a downed pine next to a clearing I startled a big black mother bear with her cub about a hundred feet away. She turned and was coming fast. I had no where to go and she wasn't slowing. Then I saw a flash of red. It was the fox heading for the cub, running into it head on, knocking it over. That cub cried out like a baby. The mother slammed on her brakes 20 feet away, turned and went back chasing the fox from the cub. You could hear her puffing through the brush after the fox. Thank God for the downed trees.

I did hear the fox yelp, hoping she had got away. I wasn't standing in my tracks either, heading back to the shack and my gun.

The next morning getting up early, gotta get the chores done. Stepping out the door I looked across the clearing, there was the mother fox and the kit sitting side by side watching me.

You know if you owe, you'd better pay up. What's a chicken---or two---once a week? Oh, hell, sitting down in my chair.

That was her sign; she ran down a chicken, limped back to the kit, looked my way and was into the woods.

~

18
The Lost Girl and the Vest

Alice, an inquisitive little girl, was just turning six. Her birthday had been on March 21. She was enjoying her summer at their large house on the Mississippi River, located on Highway 10 south of 200, thirteen miles from Jacobson. It was so large because it had been a lodging house built in the 1800's for the paddle boats plying up and down the Mississippi. It had been said some of them went as far north up the river as Grand Rapids and some times further.

She and her family had moved here a short time ago, her father wanting to get out of the Twin Cities to raise the kids in an area with less crime. Alice had an older brother, David, 14 and sister, Maya, 12.

At one time, much of the land around them had been fields; most of them now had poplar trees and heavy brush. The grass in the open field was at least knee high this time of the year. It had been a dry summer so the mosquitoes hadn't been much of a bother.

It would be nothing to see several deer in the evening. Alice had seen a bear cross the road a short distance from the house. Some times at night she could hear wolves howling. Fearing them, she would not go out after dark.

The house was up a steep hill from the river. The children were told many times not to go to the river without an adult.

The river was narrow, deep, and fast flowing, sinister at night. There had been a lot of flooding in the spring; at times you could see trees floating by.

Alice's parents, Jim and Marie had left her brother David in charge this morning, he being almost 15. They would be driving to Grand Rapids which would be 40 miles to stock up on groceries and some implements at the L & M Supply store.

Earlier that morning Alice had been playing on the hillside, it had been cool. Going up and down the hill she had taken her green jacket off, leaving it a short distance from the water knowing she was not to go close to it.

David had a small dinner for the girls, Campbell's tomato soup, crackers and toast. Everyone had a nap. Alice was up in a short time. It was clouding up so she slipped into her gray hooded sweatshirt, then onto the porch to rock in the old rocking chair that had come with the house. After a time she remembered her green jacket down by the river. She was only part way down the hill, when he started to yell at her, "Get off the hill and back up here now!"

Alice tried to tell him she was just trying to get her coat but being the big brother he was not listening. Coming up the hill, she thought, "What is the matter with him, I am not a little kid any more, I'm almost 7!"

It was close to 4:00 in the afternoon, she decided to play along the road a short distance from the house. Her feelings had been hurt by her brother and she wasn't about to forget it soon. She had been told never to cross the road but there was a little trail and a clearing in just a short distance. She could see the house and knew where she was, then getting into the clearing there was a long hill. Climbing to the top and looking down, she could see a lot of water on one side of the branches and what she thought was a dog swimming there. The dog was climbing up on the branches; it looked very funny as it had short legs and a tail that was long and flat.

Climbing down to get a closer look, the dog slid back into the water. Raising its tail, it hit the water with a loud smack. Going under, it disappeared. She waited a short time; she didn't know where it had gone.

Realizing she had been gone for some time, her brother was going to be mad. She started up the hillside, but getting on top, nothing looked familiar. Choosing a trail, she started walking thinking it led to the small clearing. After walking a short distance, she thought it must be just a little further. A little further she could see the trail ended. There was no clearing, she had missed it. She would go back the other way where she had seen the dog. After walking some distance, she couldn't find the hill.

Starting to feel scared now, she thought maybe her brother would hear if she yelled so she would walk a short distance and yell. Then listening, nothing. Thinking again, she said to herself, "I think I know what direction the house is in; I'll just go in that direction. If I hurry, I'll be out before dark."

She was getting tired; she could see the long hill a short distance in front of her. Getting to the top of it, there was no water. She had been walking over an hour or more. Looking up, the sun was getting low in the trees. The tears were starting to come, she was scared.

Listening, she thought she could hear the bell but couldn't tell which direction the sound came from. She loved that bell; it was mounted on a yoke in their yard and had come from an old steam engine. Mother never called the kids, she would just walk out, pull the handle down, let the clapper hit the side, and you could hear it for a mile.

David, after napping was busy cleaning the kitchen. He had seen Alice rocking in the chair, Maya was upstairs, his mother would be proud. He would be glad to see them; they always brought home surprise treats.

After a short time, walking over, looking out to the rocking chair, Alice wasn't in it. Glancing around the front yard, she was probably around the side of the house. He would finish the kitchen. Then he started to remember she had been going toward the river. Looking outside she couldn't be seen. Looking upstairs, yelling to Maya, "Is Alice up there?" Maya replied, "No, I haven't seen her for some time."

David started calling, "Alice, Alice," no reply. He headed for the river bank. Looking, he could see nothing. The brush and trees could be hiding her, could she be hiding from him because she was still mad at him? Going down the bank, he couldn't see her. Then he was startled, there was her green coat.

He was breathing hard; his heart was in his throat. He didn't know what to do. Going to the waters edge, walking and running along through the brush looking out over the water along the bank, nothing. Back up the hill; check out the small buildings, how long had she been gone?

He'd have to go back to the house and call his father. They had a portable downstairs, he couldn't find it. His sister, he called upstairs to Maya telling her to bring the phone down as he needed it. She replied she would bring it down shortly.

He was headed up the stairs, he needed that phone. Maya was startled the way he looked, she gave him the phone. He was telling her that Alice was missing. Check the house, every nook and cranny. She may be hiding, she was mad at him. "I'm calling Mom and Dad," David told Maya.

He was so nervous; he was punching the wrong numbers on the phone, then would have to start over. Finally getting her number in, it rang and rang, no answer. Hanging up, he remembered what she had once told him, if you think someone is in a car they may not be able to get the phone out right away. Wait a short time and than try again. This was so hard to do, waiting a couple minutes, seemed like an hour. He punched in her number again, this time she answered.

He tried to stay calm, asking where they were. She said they were just coming to Highway 200 and should be home in a few minutes, was there a problem? Taking a deep breath, it came out of him; he couldn't find his little sister. He had looked everywhere, he didn't tell her about the green jacket. Marie repeated, "Did you say everywhere?" He said, "Mom, please hurry." She told him they would be home soon,"You and your sister stay put, don't go anywhere."

It seemed like hours. Getting out of the car, trying to stay calm, Jim was asking when they had last seen Alice. Had they seen any cars on the road that could have picked her up? Had she been out by the road?

Telling them to make a sweep of all the buildings, he would drive down the road and be right back. They had come from the north so he would drive the south road. The rest of them spread out checking the out buildings, the attic, also the trunk of the old car.

In a short time, Jim was back. They had found nothing. He asked, "Had anyone checked the river?" David stepped forward; he had checked down there. What he said then, stunned them, adding he had found Alice's green coat down there but not close to the river.

Jim said, "We need some help." He was then on the phone to the Aitkin County Sheriff's office. It would take some time; none of their cars were in the area.

In the evening two sheriff's cars pulled into the driveway. One was pulling a boat. Meanwhile the parents having left David and Maya at the house were searching some tree stands close by. They were to be ringing the bell every few minutes.

David told the deputies he had found the green coat by the river but had searched the area not finding any signs of her.

The deputies told the family not much could be done due to the approaching darkness; they would be arranging search parties for the morning. Meanwhile the bell would be rung every so often. They had some search lights set up so the area would be well lit through the night. Having contact with the St. Louis County Sheriff's office, their search dogs would be there in the morning.

Jim and Marie knew there would be no sleep for them that night. As there was nothing they could do until morning, the kids were put to bed. Marie went to her bedroom and when Jim looked in the young girl was on her knees next to the bed. She was down early the next morning making coffee and breakfast for the deputies.

Alice had never liked the dark, she was so scared. It was getting dark now; she knew they would be out looking for her. She could hear the bell in the distance, not being able to tell from what direction.

She was happy she had worn her tennis shoes, jeans and hooded sweatshirt. The mosquitoes were starting to bother her but only a few of them.

She had been following deer trails; it was getting too dark to see. She came to a small pine tree with needles around the bottom and a lot of long grass, she was so tired. She crept under the bows leaning against the tree. She knew she would be spending the dark night alone. As she sat there in the quiet of the night, she could see the stars in the sky and thought they were the brightest she'd ever seen in her life.

Looking over the tree tops, a full moon. Alice said to herself, "Mother must have prayed for that so I wouldn't be in the dark."

She knew she was tired; her feet were wet though the night was rather warm. She drifted off and the next thing she knew something was walking close to her. She could see a mother deer and a little fawn. They stopped and then moved on. She could see it was getting light in one direction. After a short time it was a blazing orange. She didn't know what to do. Thinking I had better sit still for a while, she could hear the bell, but from where?

Throughout the day she had seen a helicopter and a small airplane go over several times. Maybe they were looking for her? It was in the early afternoon she could hear some hounds baying in the distance, never close.

She was awfully thirsty. There had been a lot of water the day before, she would find some. In a short time she found a small creek by one of the long, tall hills. It was getting close to dark again. This would be her second night alone.

Jim had told all the deputies about the green coat being found by the river, boats would be working the river today, not knowing how they would do because of the fast currant. If she was in the water she could be some distance away by now. Searches would be made of the land across the road. Jim also told them about that land, how he thought the WPA many years ago had dredged deep long ditches to drain the water. This made 15 foot hills several miles long with waterways next to them. These ditches were probably a half mile apart. Through the years, brush and trees had grown on them making it difficult now for their parties to search. Beaver had dammed up many of the ditches.

The deputies had organized well. First they sent the dogs with the handlers; a helicopter was overhead along with an airplane. Search parties were organized and given areas to search. As the day wore on there was never any sign or good news. Everyone was thinking the river. More boats were brought in. It seemed hopeless. This would be Alice's second night without being found. If she wasn't in the river, where was she?

Marie had cried herself out. When she had the time, could be seen next to the bed on her knees.

Their bedroom was on the second floor, they could see the river on one side, the main road on the other. She would spend some time looking at the river then back at the main road. Across the main road she could see the little trail going back to the clearing and the long hill in the distance; this is going to be another long night.

Alice was very hungry; she had been able to find water and was tired. She wasn't so scared now, someone would find her soon. Looking for a tree like the night before with pine needles, she could stay a little warmer. It was cooling off, tonight would be colder. Walking along, she picked up a four foot long stick to help her balance. She saw what she was looking for, a shaggy tree with lots of pine needles under it. Crawling under, scraping the needles together to sit on. Leaning on the tree, she looked up and there was Mother's moon, oh, how that comforted her. She knew Mother would pray, Dad would be out searching, Dad would find her.

It had been a long night for Alice, she had shivered most it. Not getting much sleep, feeling weaker, her knees hurt from falling down so many times. The stick she was carrying helped to keep her balance.

The sun started to come up, the sky turned a brilliant orange again. The warmth that came with it, soon she was asleep again. It was in the afternoon before she was fully awake. She was feeling weaker. Off in a distance she could see one of those long, high hills; she would try to make it before dark. She didn't want to spend a third night in the woods.

Jim was out with the deputies, having only a couple hours of sleep. They had searched everywhere. It appeared to be hopeless. At the end of this day, most of the search parties would be gone. No one thought a little girl would make it without food and water, the nights getting colder.

The search parties had gone out but as the day wore on, they had been coming back tired and worn out. The rough terrain had gotten to most of them.

As they were getting into their cars, Jim went to each deputy, thanking them personally. The day had gone by so fast. This would be his third night without his little daughter. Thinking, some times you don't know what you have until you lose it.

As Alice started for the long hill she was using her stick for balance. She knew she was moving slowly, trying to use the deer trails going in her direction. As she came to a Y in the trail, she was happy to see a young dog looking at her. It was quite furry and gray seeming to have yellow eyes. It held its head low. Taking a step toward her, she could feel the hair tighten on the back of her head. A chill was going up her spine. Moving forward and showing its fangs. Suddenly she raised her stick, taking a couple steps forward, slamming the stick into the ground all this time screeching at the top of her lungs, all of her frustrations of the last couple days coming out. The animal yelped, took off skirting through the trees. She fell forward starting to cry.

Having had her cry, she got up even more determined, taking her stick heading for the hill. It was dark when she struggled to its top. Sitting down for a breather, looking up, there was a tall young man dressed all in orange. He had the nicest smile, yellow hair and striking blue eyes.

There seemed to be an aura of light all around him. Looking at her, he said, "Alice, I've come to help you, are you ready to go home?" "Yes, I'm so cold and thirsty." He gave her a cup of water, the sweetest she'd ever known. Taking off his orange vest, wrapping it around her, it was very big but seemed to fit. It was so light and warm.

Taking her hand, saying we have a long way to go and so little time for me. Feeling his hand; it was so warm, almost like electricity, "What is your name?" "It's Gabriel, is that alright?" "Yes."

As they walked, she seemed so much lighter on her feet, seeming to draw strength from the young man. They were walking on deer trails on the long hill. It seemed they had walked for hours. The light seemed to be getting dimmer.

At last they were stopping on the top of the hill. Looking down, you could see the water, the branches with the short legged dog sitting there.

Taking her by the shoulders, he turned her around; she could see the clearing and their house across the road. The lights were on, she heard the bell.

Starting down the hill, he seemed to be faltering. Making their way through the clearing, then onto the little trail, the light was fading, she started to get weaker. Could she make the road? On the edge of the ditch she started to fall. There was a flash of light; she was on the road standing. Gabriel was gone.

Marie was on her knees by the bed. A light entered the bedroom, looking out through the window, in an aura of light stood a man on the hill in the trees. Then they were descending, a child by his side. She knew she was dreaming but she couldn't take her eyes away. As they got closer the light was getting dimmer. Next to the road there was a flash and the man was gone. Standing in the road was a young girl in an orange vest.

She knew and was running down the stairs through the yard across the road. Grabbing, hugging her girl who looked so tired.

Jim had seen none of this. He had been looking to the lost river, hearing the door slam, Marie running across the road then he saw her too.

Marie could never hear this story from Alice often enough, for in her heart she knew.

Jim often wondered how she found her way home in the dark that night and where she had found the orange vest.

From that night on, the vest was always in Alice's room.

Alice, 23 now, is working as a nurse in orphanages, helping others. She is visiting this week, bringing home a young man she is in love with, a tall blond with the bluest eyes you have ever seen.

Looking, you can see she is walking him over to look at the dogs on the beaver dam. The orange vest fits him perfectly. His name is Gabriel.

~

19
Through the Valley

Sarah is on the road to the Grand Rapids Hospital.

The young man she had been intimate with a few years ago had called her from Denver, Colorado saying his parents were now gone, he was alone. Asking her if she would see him again as he had never forgotten the short time they had been together.

That phone call was all it took to rekindle the flame that had been theirs. Now there were to be many phone calls between the two young lovers talking about how they had met at a Remer Days celebration.

How Tim had walked up to the vendor, ordering a hot dog, taking a bite, then reaching into his pocket to pay for it. Then patting and reaching into his pockets realizing he had left his billfold back in his car. Feeling his face getting redder, stuttering to the vendor, "I..I--"

The copper haired girl with freckles handed a $5 bill to pay for the hot dog, also buying them a bottle of pop. Then they were walking over, sitting on a bench in front of the meat market which long ago had once been the only theater in town with a marquee still above their heads.

They would sit and watch the Remer Days Parade go by not saying much at first. Then as Tim cast his eye at Sarah, he could see the dimples, the sides of her mouth working, she couldn't hold it any longer, she had just taken a drink and it was all over his shirt and pants. They were both laughing so hard, people were staring, some of them breaking into laughter as well.

As he sat there looking he could see she had the greenest eyes, a big mouth with beautiful teeth, guessing she was about 18. That was good because he had just turned 20. Then she reached out her hand to him saying, "My name is Sarah Jean Long and you be?"

Taking her hand, it was warm and strong, he was flustered, saying, "Tim Dung, I mean Duncan." And, she was laughing again.

Tim didn't know what was wrong with him, he had always been so assured, good in all sports, and this was not like him.

For the size of Remer, it was a long lasting parade and the only thing big about Remer was the wide street through town and the big red brick firehouse on the west side of town. From where they sat they could see to the west, the old train depot, a two story, long yellow building with the tracks running through town going east toward Shovel Lake and in the distance the town's water tower.

Then Sarah was saying, "Let me show you the town." Tim thought, "That will only take five minutes." But there were things he hadn't seen, a flea market west by the railroad tracks, that took an hour to browse through, and then they were walking to the other side of town to the little park. There was a tent to eat in and a stage with some pretty good singing. As they were walking towards the tent, he was holding Sarah's hand. She looked up grinning.

Entering the tent Sarah bought them a pulled pork sandwich and a pop. He was telling her he would be paying her back. Then he told her he was a runner and would be running in the 10k at 9:30 the next morning, Sunday. To his surprise he discovered she was already signed up for it too.

It was getting into the early evening; Sarah thought if he had a car she could show him the rest of the town. Taking her by the hand, he led her north past the church a block. Pointing to a 1968 red Mustang convertible, she was mildly surprised. It was an older car in showroom condition. He explained he worked for the L&M Supply in Grand Rapids and had his own money.

She had him drive to the old brick schoolhouse pointing out where she lived in a white house just across the street with a little white camper trailer sitting next to the garage.

They were on County Road 4 driving south past the yellow depot and, in a short time, they were coming to a little cemetery just ahead on their left. She had him drive in on the second drive-way saying some of her family was buried here. Coming to the next corner she had him stop. She pointed to two little headstones side by side. You could see the year 1939 on them.

Sarah began to tell Tim about the story of the two little boys buried there. In 1939 they lived in a big two story house across the tracks in the south part of town, the Peabody house. Somehow with the two little boys alone in the house, it caught fire. A crowd was standing outside; you could hear the boys' screams. A woman named Hazel who lived close by seemed to come out of nowhere, rushed into the house followed closely by her brother, Earl. Soon they were bringing out two badly burned boys. Then standing, holding the crying children until an ambulance arrived; they were then rushed to the hospital in Grand Rapids. It is said, they were asking for ice cream. Both of the boys died later in the day. Hazel then returned home. Her children could see her coming across the field in great pain, holding her burned and blistered hands up as she approached them a doctor later came and applied salve on her hands arms and chest. She was in pain for some time.

"Even our little towns have past histories and stories," explained Sarah.

Then she had him driving east along side the railroad tracks. This looked like it could be the seediest part of town. Abandoned cars, grass two to three feet high, unkempt yards. Soon they were leaving town on the old dirt road, the tracks on their right. About a half mile out of town, she pointed to something of interest. Across the tracks and a field was an old caved-in log cabin. It had certainly seen better days. She was telling Tim, old houses, especially log houses intrigued her, who had lived there, what they were like, the stories they could tell.

Now they were coming to where the road turned right crossing over the tracks, you could see three long buildings coming on your left. They were very old and in disrepair. On your right was an abandoned two story house set back in the pine trees, some very large and over 100 years old. She explained to Tim this was the old Reasoner turkey farm of many years ago, possibly the 1930's. Parking, he came around the car to help her out (like she needed it!), but this would be the perfect time. As he opened the door, taking her hand helping her up and out, they stood breathtakingly close facing each other. A twinkle in his eyes, and so good looking, she knew this was the moment they both had been waiting for. He slowly leaned over looking deeply into her wanting eyes, then kissing the back of her hand, leading her to the old house.

What a dufus, she knew you could lead a horse to water but you can't make him drink. Well, she would see about that.

As they approached the house, you could see many of the windows were broken. There was a front porch, the steps were gone. Tim jumped up, turning to help her up as he pulled on her hands she jumped coming up faster than he expected. He was falling over backwards. Sarah landed fully on him. Face to face, Tim didn't know what to do looking up at her.

Those green eyes of Sarah's inches away staring into his, not moving her body off of his, and then her mouth was on his, gently at first then demanding. Her legs were astraddle of him, he couldn't get out. He didn't want out; his arms came around her pulling her tighter. Sarah thought, "What am I doing, I want this man now, this may be my first time but he's not getting away from me."

Tim was fully aroused at this copper haired tiger on him, he had wanted her too not expecting it to be on a broken down porch. Soon they were coming together. Tim was very gentle, suspecting it was her first time.

Exploring the old house seemed to have been forgotten.

After a short time, it was getting quite dark and much colder. As she laid her head on his shoulder, he could feel the cold run through her.

Then Tim was saying, "I don't know why I didn't think of this sooner but I called last night and have a room reserved at the little Remer Motel so I wouldn't have to get up early for the run tomorrow. I could drive you home or we could be more comfortable there." Sarah sat up and looking at him said, "Aren't you the bright one, I hope it has a soft bed."

Getting up, rearranging their clothes, they were soon in the convertible driving back into Remer. Looking over, her hand on his shoulder, "Won't your parents be worried about you?" "I'll call Mom and tell her I'm having fun with some friends, she'll be alright, I am 18 and a big girl now!" looking into his eyes.

They were soon at the Remer Motel. He went in, getting the keys to Unit 7. He brought his bag in setting it on the floor.

Sarah went over sitting on the soft bed thinking, "I hope I wasn't too easy and this isn't a one night stand, but if it is, he is a fantastic lover, I'll always remember this day and night if I live to be a hundred."

Tim came over setting on the bed beside her. She started to

remove a few things then scooted up laying her head on a pillow, waiting.

At a quarter to three, she said, "Maybe you should drive me home; we have the 10K run at 9:30." Then she was up trying to get the wrinkles out of her clothes. Slipping them on and into the bathroom, a little lipstick, trying to get a comb through her hair, looking into the mirror that was going to have to do. Mother should be in bed when I get home.

Tim had been standing there waiting thinking that even when they are in a hurry it takes them a long time.

Getting into the little convertible, she reached over putting her hand on his leg as they drove the short distance to her house. Pulling up, he came around to help her out. As she came up and out, coming together he knew what to do this time.

Sarah was saying they would meet at the tent in the little park at 8:30 the next morning. Later in the day she would have a little surprise thing for them to do.

As he was kissing her goodnight, looking through the front door glass, a movement, a door closing across the room.

Sarah was soon hugging up to her pillow. Then she started to think like a normal woman. For a young man, he showed a lot of experience. Smiling, she drifted off.

Tim was into bed thinking, "I never dreamed I could find a woman like this. So alluring, so beautiful in a small town like Remer. All day, I had wanted to kiss her, I couldn't find the courage, and then it happened. I couldn't write this in a story book and make this more beautiful - copper hair, green eyes and a body to dream about. But, her wit and charm was what really brought me to her." As he was drifting off to sleep, he thought, "I'm really beat."

Waking a couple minutes after 8:00, jumping out of bed. "I'm going to have to hurry to see her at 8:30." Getting his running gear and shoes on, he was out the door approaching the sign-in tent; there she was, drop dead gorgeous in her tight green running shorts and bra. As he approached her, he asked, "How did you sleep?" With a grin, "She replied, like a log with some very nice dreams!" "You?" Raising his eyebrows, "Like never before!"

Then it was watching the hustle and bustle as kids and grownups were signing up for the races. You could see teams already playing basketball down a block on the corner with makeshift basket hoops.

The 10K'ers were the first to line up. There were around 25 of them. The gun was going off.

At first Tim tried to set a pace that he thought Sarah could hold. They were turning the corner on Hwy 4 running north and they would be going by the cemetery they had been to last night.

They were in the lead pack. Looking at Sarah, she looked very relaxed, matching him stride for stride. Perhaps he could set the pace a little faster. She along with four others was out in front of everyone else. Tim knew he was a good runner, this was a fast pace. How long could she stay with him? Then they were turning at the halfway point, three other runners and Sarah made the turn together. A man about 35 in a red shirt quickened his pace getting out 8-10 feet ahead. Tim could see he was good falling in behind him. Sarah had been next to him disappeared. Then hearing something behind him, he knew she was close behind drafting. Where had she learned that? Now they were by the graveyard again in a few blocks, they would be turning left with a quarter mile to go. Red shirt was now out 30 feet, Sarah behind him somewhere. Then they made a right turn, a block to go. Pushing hard he would be at least second. Someone was by his side, he couldn't believe it, and she beat him across the finish line by five feet!

He was about to learn that she held some school records for the Remer School track team. He was standing there bent over trying to catch his breath. There she was grinning, starting to laugh, he wanted to but how do you laugh when you are out of breath?

They sat around talking to some of the runners she knew. Red shirt, who turned out to have been Sarah's track coach, came over and shook his hand telling Tim how well he had done and got a big hug from Sarah. After a short time, he walked over and picked up something to drink, sitting down, trying to cool down. It was a hot day.

Sarah said, "Tim, I was telling you last night I have a wonderful surprise for you, Mother and I have made up a picnic basket. We can pick it up around noon, I'm going to show you my favorite spot on Willow Lake, and it's marvelous." Looking into his eyes, she said, "Maybe we should walk to your place to get the car and your swimming suit."

At that time, Tim swallowed trying to say something, nothing came out. Taking her by the hand, squeezing it, they started for the motel somewhat hurriedly. They entered the motel room; Tim went over pulling his swim trunks from his luggage. Turning there she was like the day she was born waiting for him, walking over, he picked her up and they were lovers again. Laying her down softly, he came to her; they only had a short time. Soon they were quite proper driving soon to meet Sarah's parents.

Jean, Sarah's mother, met them at the door, inviting them in. He was almost startled, they looked so much alike. Coming across the room, her father, Don, put out his hand. Looking at him, he could see where Sarah got her athletic abilities. They were very pleasant.

In just a short time, Sarah had changed her clothes and was carrying things from the kitchen loading Tim up with food to take to the car and a big blanket to set and eat upon. She had a nice outfit on, her swimsuit under it.

As they pulled from the curb, Sarah was waving to her mother standing in the doorway with a knowing look on her face. Soon they were driving east on Hwy 6 in the direction of Willow Lake which was about eight miles away.

As you turn off to Willow Lake onto a dirt road, driving down a steep hill, the lake is spread out below you through the trees. The sun above you, the refraction of the silver is so bright off the foot high waves like a billion shards of broken glass all shifting in a constant dance of unforgettable beauty. Part way down, they stopped the car trying to take it all in.

On the far side of the lake where wind cannot touch the lake, the flat glass water reflects the tall jade pine trees. Nature's wondrous painting on the water, a sight with the serenity of the moment.

They park on the shore of the lake, top down on the convertible, she is telling him of the many times she has been here. Always remembering the glittering glass of the lake as they come down through the trees and of the time her church had a school bus driven here years ago. Almost all of the church members had gone out into the lake, tipped over backwards and baptized with their clothes on.

Soon they were out walking the beach in their swimsuits holding hands, then testing the water ankle deep. A little deeper and she was under the water in a beautiful arrythematic stroke, coming up perhaps a hundred feet away. He was swimming to meet her, coming close he was met with a heavy splash in the face and she was under again. That's how the next hour went. Finally they were spreading the blanket on the grass, laying there admiring each other. Both a little tired from the last hour's water battles, enjoying the quietness of the moment in the warm sun.

Then they were bringing out the lunch basket; potato salad, beans, hot dogs (still warm), pickles and bread along with bottles of cold root beer.

It turned into a wonderful afternoon to lie on the blanket and enjoy the sun and tell about each other. Finding they could go for half an hour and not say anything, just the other one being there.

Then it happened, her halter just seemed to fall away, lying there looking at him, those green eyes and a smile inviting him. He lay there for some time admiring the beauty of this creature before him, then reaching over and taking her hand pulling her to him, kissing face, neck and body, she with both of her hands in his hair. It was into the evening, you could see a blood red moon reflecting off the flat surface of the lake.

A little out of breath, they were sitting close face to face, legs entwined holding hands. Shortly, Sarah said, "You seem troubled like there is something you want to say." He just sat there. "She was saying, look, if it's something about the last couple days, you don't owe me anything. No promises have been made, whatever may happen I will always remember what we shared between us."

Tim was looking into her eyes, squeezing her hand saying, "I should have told you this much sooner. Both Mom and Dad are in very poor health and are moving to Colorado next week hoping the climate will help them. I am through with my job next Friday at the L&M Supply store and will be going with them as they need my help. I never expected to meet someone like you and what will happen with them over the next few years, I have no idea."

"My folks taught me to respect and not take advantage of anyone. Don't think badly of me, you are my first and I have no excuse. Those green eyes looking into mine, I couldn't resist, I wanted you more than anything in my life," he continued. "Most of all, I wanted to please. "

"Nothing will ever take these few days from me; they are something I will always treasure. We are both so young so much life to live. I can't make any promises; I feel so lost on what I'm trying to say."

There were a few tears on Sarah's face too. She was thinking no promises, no regrets over the last few days. What ever happens in the future, I'll have my memories to fall back on.

It was late evening; someone was watching two lovers through the shades, saying their goodbyes. Their hands couldn't seem to part. The girl was running to the house. A bedroom door was quickly shut; the girl coming in went directly to her room.

The boy driving home that night made the turn down to Willow Lake, sitting and admiring it, thinking, "I have nothing to offer a girl like Sarah. She will always be with me." It was early morning when he arrived home.

By the end of the week all traces the Duncans had ever lived here were gone.

It had been somewhat of a surprise to Sarah when she had received the first call from Tim Duncan after almost three years. She had written him off but had secretly hoped. She had realized the great responsibly he would have with very sick parents and thought she understood.

Now over the last month they had talked many times over the phone. He had almost everything taken care of, the house had been sold and there was some life insurance from the parents.

Tim had noticed that although they talked openly as lovers, when asked about her everyday life, it was like she seemed to get vague. Speaking openly about her job at the school but then what did he expect? What had he done to earn her confidence?

One day Tim called saying he was leaving the next day, Saturday morning and should be in early Sunday.

Sarah was beside herself. She didn't think it would be like this. Her mother was saying, "What's the matter with you? He hurt you badly before."

Sunday morning the family had gone to church. Coming home, Sarah was thinking, "It won't be long now." Early afternoon, no phone call. No word into the evening. Sarah didn't sleep well that night. Monday morning she was getting ready for work. Her mother looking worried, saying, "It's for the better."

Nothing on Tuesday. Wednesday morning the faculty was sitting around having their coffee. A man said when I gassed up in Hill City this morning, there was this wrecked red Mustang convertible, nothing but scrap now sitting in back of the station. They were sure beautiful old cars. It seems a pulpwood truck lost its breaks on 200 going through the stop sign on 169, rolling that Mustang down the road in front of it. About last Sunday I guess.

Someone had spilled her coffee; she looked to be in a daze, almost falling over her chair. She didn't seem to know which way to turn and Sarah was saying, "I'm terribly sick, I have to go home." Someone was trying to help, brushing them aside, stumbling out the door.

Getting in her car, she drove home and was soon telling her mother what she had just heard, saying she was driving to Hill City as it was only 18 miles and had to know all that had happened. Jean, her mother, said, "I'll take care of everything here, just let me know." And she gave Sarah a hug.

Sarah was pushing it. Thank God, Hwy 200 was such a straight road. Coming to Hill City, stopping at the stop sign, she could see and recognized what was left of Tim's car, thinking, "No one lives through that."

Going into the station, questioning people, no one seemed to know much. Then barging into the office, she was talking to the manager, asking about the car.

"Yes," he seemed to want to talk about it. He was outside about 11:00 Sunday morning when he heard this horn, looking up he could see the big pulp wood truck blow through the stop sign blowing his horn, coming across 169. The red car was flying through the air, rolling; a man flew out into the ditch rolling over and over. The truck stopped down the road a ways, seems he lost his brakes.

"I ran over to the car driver, not much you could do for him," the man told Sarah. "Wasn't long and a lot of highway men and a sheriff's deputy was here and an ambulance from the Rapids."

Sarah asked, "Was the car driver still alive?"

The man replied, "Well, there sure were a lot of excited people!"

Sarah looked him in the eye and said, "Damnit, was the driver still alive?"

The man looked startled, saying, "If he was, it won't be for long." Sarah had heard him say an ambulance from the Rapids.

Sarah, left the shop, walked out to the mangled Mustang. There were some maps and clothing in disarray spread about the car. She noticed the glove compartment was still closed. The car door was sprung open. Opening the glove box she was surprised to find several pictures of herself taken the day she had spent with Tim. He must have gotten them from the newspaper as one of them was of them coming across the finish line of the 10K race. There was also a photo of her standing in the water at Willow Lake; she hadn't seen him with a camera that afternoon. There were car registrations, car insurance, and other personal papers. Studying them, she now had his full name, date of birth and his address in Colorado.

Sarah was now on the road to the Grand Rapids Hospital and thinking, I've been to hospitals before and they have rules. If you are not the wife or close relative, they are not allowed to give you any information on a patient. What am I going to do? There has to be a way. A thought came to her. Pulling into the parking lot and going through her purse she found some cheap rings. Thinking, these should do it. She slipped them on her ring finger. Putting the papers from the glove box into her purse, she approached the front desk. Putting out her left hand so a flash of the rings could be seen, saying, "I'm Mrs. Tim Duncan, I came as fast as I could. What room is my husband in?" And then she just started to lose it and was crying.

The receptionist knew who she was talking about right away, saying that Mr. Duncan was in ICU. She could give no information but could have her escorted to the ICU.

They were approaching Tim's room; the nurse could understand what Sarah was going through. Taking her into Room 15, he was hard to recognize. The nurse said he was in a coma in very critical condition. Sarah could recognize some of the equipment, oxygen, feeding tubes, a cardiac machine. The nurse added, "When he was brought in unconscious, his case was taken immediately by one of the best trauma doctors in the state, a Dr. Rajala, who will be with us for three months. The doctor will be on his rounds in a couple hours. There are soft chairs for family; I really wish I could help you more. If you need me, there is a call button."

There was a phone in the room. Sarah was able to get an outside line, calling her mother in Remer, telling her where she was and what she had learned about the accident, how she claimed to be married to gain access to see Tim. He was in a coma and didn't look good; she would be talking to a doctor soon. She would be calling in on her job requesting emergency leave due to illness and asking her mother if they could handle everything that was going on there. She replied, "I'm sure your dad and I can."

At 3:00 Dr. Rajala, the surgeon walked in. A good looking middle-aged man, reached out his hand and introduced himself, saying, "I'm glad you are here. Tim has been here three days and we didn't know if he had any relatives.

"The situation doesn't look good, he has a fractured left arm and ribs, internal injuries and head trauma.

"He is now in a coma, that is a medical emergency and attention must first be directed to maintaining the patient's respiration and circulation using intubation and ventilation, administrations of intervenience fluids or blood as needed and other supportive care and the neck stabilized."

He said, "I know this is a lot to take in, but we have a different test to give us a clue to the seriousness of what we have. The coma was caused by the accident which would be called anatomic and these cases of coma are diagnosed from CT (computed tomography) scans or MRI's (magnetic resonance imagining).

"Then we have other ways to help us measure what the final outcome may be. None of this is infallible. One of them is called the Glasgow coma scale, a system to examining a comatose patient for evaluating the depth of the comas tracking progress and predicting the ultimate outcome. This scale runs from 1-15. There are three categories, 1-3 of course, are very bad, a 3-5 patient score often suggest he has likely suffered fatal brain damage, 8 or more points are getting better, we think Tim at the moment is 7. This is not an exact science. I wish I could be more precise. If you need anything, please let me know, this could be a long process."

Sarah stood looking at Tim for some time, she could see he had matured under the black and blue and was the man she had fallen in love with so long ago. Now taking his hand and saying a prayer. The doctor had indirectly told her there isn't much of a chance; she would be there until the end.

This was to be the beginning of their ordeal together. She would be alternating her time with Tim, one day morning until late afternoon, the next day, afternoon until late at night as she had other responsibilities. The first few days, just talking to him, then she was bringing books, sitting reading *Gulliver's Travels*, *Moby Dick*, *Riders of the Purple Sage* by Zane Grey.

At this time, the doctor was saying that the internal injuries maybe were taking their toll. It had been almost two weeks. There were no signs that he was coming out of the coma.

In the early hours of the evening, Sarah knew the end was coming near. Very softly she was reading her Bible.

Tim's mind, coming from a deep, deep sleep, thought, "Where am I, why can't I wake up?"

Trying to move his head, it was not moving. "What are those words I am hearing, they're not very clear. Who? The voice? 'He trust in the Lord, let the Lord rescue him. Let Him deliver him, He delights in him.'" Then Tim was back into his dark world of sleep.

Awake, but not awake, Tim heard a nurse say it may be a few days. "Now don't they know I can hear them?" He thought. "This heavy fog that comes and goes, open my eyes, look around me, nothing. Time is flying, I can tell as they come and go. My eyes aren't opening, what is wrong?"

Slowly, it is coming together, for him. He understands he's in a hospital, and he is going to die. Laying there in his prison of silence, he is helpless. There is a rage building within, "Why can't they listen?"

Then, someone is reading to him. "The Lord is my shepherd, I shall not be in want," she reads. "He makes me lie down in green pastures, he leads me beside quiet waters, he restores my soul. He guides me in paths of righteousness for his name's sake. Even though I walk through the valley of the shadow of death, I will fear no evil, for you are with me; your rod and your staff, they comfort me."

Tim's rage seems to soften with those words, the voice he has been hearing, soft and peaceful.

"You prepare a table before me in the presence of my enemies. You anoint my head with oil; my cup overflows," she continues.

"Surely goodness and love will follow me all the days of my life, and I will dwell in the house of the Lord forever."

Sarah, standing over Tim, finishing the Psalms of David. Looking down, she could see his eyelids move ever so slowly, just a reaction or a sign?

Sarah, holding his hand, looking onto his face was saying, "As you lie there during your darkening hours, I will be your rainbow of light. I will be walking with you through what was our short time together, our love of forever."

In a few days, she takes him back to a night of some years ago, telling him of a young copper haired girl who had found her true love on a broken down porch, how they had gotten married, had two children, Timothy and Jean. And oh, they were twins, both copper haired. Each day she was adding to the story.

Dreading the ending for she knew what it was.

Then, one morning, Sarah walked into the hospital room into the bluest set of eyes and a very weak smile! Running over, she instantly had her arms around him with insufferable sobs she could not control.

Looking up, Dr, Rajala was standing there with a smile on his face telling her, "If you remember, I told you none of these predictions were infallible. A few prayers and someone reaching down into their souls, giving them the will to live, you've done that. His recovery is remarkable, now the real work will begin. It will be slow at first but his heart is there."

Smiling, the doctor looked down at Sarah's hand, and said, "You two may want to get new rings!"

Two weeks went by and Sarah had talked the doctor into allowing her to take Tim on a little excursion. Maybe a couple surprises. Sarah could scarcely contain herself.

She was there to pick him up at 10 a.m., Easter Sunday. He could see a blanket and a small basket in the back seat. She wasn't fooling him. Not saying anything, they were driving toward Remer. He was still weak.

It had been raining a light warm rain, as they turned onto a road down to Willow Lake. Starting to clear, the sun breaking through a double rainbow encompassing the lake, he said, "Do you think this is a sign of us starting over?"

The sun was breaking through the trees onto the crystal lake. They drove by a little white camper trailer and the car by it.

Then they were setting by the picnic table marveling at the double rainbow and what it meant to them, looking to his right, standing by Sarah, was a little copper haired girl saying, "Momma." He didn't know what to say. He was pointing to himself; Sarah was nodding her "Yes, saying her name is Jean." He said, She looks just like you." Then he felt someone pulling at his left sleeve, looking down, he almost fainted. A little copper haired boy with blue eyes was looking up to him saying, "Who are you?" Twins, he couldn't help himself, the tears were rolling down on his face. This was his bad arm but he managed to pull the boy to him. Sarah was saying, "His name is Timothy" and wide eyed little Jean was coming to him.

Tim was thinking of a passage he had heard a short time ago: "Surely goodness and love will follow me all the days of my life, and I will dwell in the house of the Lord forever."

~

20
The Velvet Slippers

The Paradises, John and Lisa, were still in mourning. Their daughter, Holly Ann, had been born on Christmas Day. They were getting on in years, they had tried for years and now this blessed event. Such a beautiful baby

Taking her home a few days later, she seemed to be healthy, smiling, cooing and stealing their hearts. Some time had gone by, Lisa was noticing that Holly didn't want to be fed and was losing weight. It didn't take her long to get the baby ready leaving their little house next to the Old Soldier's Cemetery.

A few minutes to the hospital next to the river, going to the back, they were ushered into a room. The doctor was soon with them asking a lot of questions, checking the baby's vital signs. At last saying the baby seemed normal, he could find nothing wrong. They were sent home, if she was still acting this way not eating, acting lethargic the next day they were to bring her in for more testing. Getting Holly home, she accepted her 6:00 feeding. Put into her crib, seemingly very content and falling asleep. Lisa was checking the baby quite often. About 10:00 she thought she was too quiet. Picking her up, she was not breathing. John who had some training from his work was trying to resuscitate her. Lisa had called the ambulance and it was there in a short time. Arriving at the hospital and taken to the emergency room, the doctor and nurses worked for an hour finally saying they had tried everything. It was listed as a crib death.

It was getting on to early March, Lisa and John had gone to church. After church it had become a ritual for them, driving to the cemetery to sit and look for a few minutes. Then Lisa had her cry while driving back to their empty house.

As John was driving his car up the driveway into his two stall garage he noticed some car prints in the snow, they hadn't been there before. Wondering who had been here while they had been to church. Also the storm door was not closed. Noting he had pulled it tight when leaving.

Approaching the door, Lisa was turning pale. Looking at him, she said, "I hear a baby crying!" Opening the door, it was hard for them to understand, a baby girl sat in the middle of the living room with chairs on their sides so she could not crawl through them.

She appeared to be about six months old, dark hair, brown eyes, light brown skin, wearing small velvet slippers and crimson velvet dress. She stopped crying, starting to smile, raising her arms to them. Lisa, reaching over the chairs picked her up. Looking at the clothing and slippers, she had never seen anything like them. She could see they had been home made with some of the finest hand stitching she had ever seen. Looking close, she could see the baby had some bruises on her arms and legs as well as the side of her face, saying, "John, come here and look at these bruises." They seem to have been made recently, showing him the velvet slippers, hand made but of the highest quality, every stitch just perfect, the same with the crimson dress. Only the finest of seamstress could have done this quality of work.

John was saying we should be calling the police, Lisa said, "Not yet, I want to see something first, taking the baby into the bedroom, laying her on the bed, taking off everything but her diaper. The baby had bruises over much of her. Lisa noticed something else very strange, the dress and slippers were of the highest quality but the diaper seemed to be made of the same design and material as comes with flour sacks although that was very common now days.

Lisa said, "John, I think someone's trying to protect this child, maybe having read of us losing ours, let's wait a day and see what happens, perhaps the mother will come back." Then John saying, "Look at this little note with writing on it next to the sink." The note read, "I hope my little Rose-wing will be free to fly, my shadow will cover the moon." The note was damp for some reason.

Before calling the police, Lisa and John talked it over. They would do everything they could to keep the child. A day later the police were called. It was a small department; it was the next day before they showed up. Saying they had no way of taking care of a child, they would notify the welfare office. In the meantime, local sheriff's offices would be called to see if a child was missing.

A lady from the welfare department showed up the next day and agreed that they may keep the child a short time until the parents could be found.

Time was passing; they had been to court, awarded temporary custody. They had taken little Rose to see a doctor. After an examination he declared the girl had been mistreated, these findings presented to the court.

Lisa had been hurt deeply loosing her own child, now she had a chance to help someone else. Looking at Rose with her light brown skin, dark hair and eyes, she suspected a white father and an Indian mother. Remembering the note she had kept. Was the note saying, "When my shadow is on the moon, I will be watching you? Meaning, Rose?" Lisa oft times felt someone was watching her.

Rose was an even tempered girl but strong willed and yes, the word was smart.

John had fallen in love with her. There was a time when someone came to the door and they thought it would be bad news. The word had gone out but no one had any information on a missing child.

Shortly after Rose had been with them, Lisa took the slippers and other clothing including the cloth diaper; put them in a paper bag. Opening the bottom drawer, they would be safe there until Rose could see them when the time was right.

Rose was with them almost a year when the court declared her abandoned. The Paradise's could now start adoption proceedings. They decided to take Rose to Costello's ice cream place and celebrate.

Each night on their knees, with Rose to say her prayers, the couple was always thanking the Lord for their good fortune.

It was almost too soon, they were driving Rose to the first grade at the down town grade school, oft times walking across the street to Johnson's grocery and buying her a snack. As she was going through grade school she was becoming very athletic and with the light brown skin, some said striking. At the end of the school day, she would come home always running to Dad first, giving him a hug, then to Lisa in the kitchen, hugging her and hanging on her wanting to help, to learn something about cooking.

Around this time they found they had a problem. Rose was into grade school, was well liked, her friends were all having birthday parties and were asking Rose when they would be invited to hers. Lisa, after a lot of thought came up with March 21st the first day of spring, a day when the sun starts to bring new life to the world as

Rose had to theirs.

As Rose was growing up, Lisa had seen tenderness in her; if an animal was hurt, a friend was sick, almost instinctively she would be there trying to help. Remembering the beatings she must have had to endure before coming to them, was there something in her mind she could remember at an early age, a built in instinct?

As she was maturing, it became clear the woods were her domain. At first walking the trails with her father, snowshoeing and skiing, wherever they were she knew where home was.

In the summer there were a few road races in the area, the 4th of July, perhaps Hill City. Entering, she would always out class the girls, coming in the lead pack with the boys, looking like she could do it again. She was getting where the boys were starting to show some interest I her. She really didn't notice.

Rose was getting into her teens now and had never approached her mother or father on how or why they had adopted her. Lisa had felt it coming for some time. One evening, they were just finishing the kitchen, Rose said, "Mom, Dad, I don't want to hurt you but I think it's time we sat down and you can tell me how you became my parents."

Sitting down by the kitchen table, the story was told, how they had tried to have a child for many years, then Holly Ann had been born to them, she had only been with us a short time before God had taken her home. We were devastated, never thinking we would be blessed again. Then an answer to a prayer, coming home on a Sunday after church, there you were crying on our living room floor. Someone, we suspect your mother, had made a corral with chairs on their sides so you couldn't get out. You were clean but it was obvious there was a lot of bruising on you, we felt at the time your mother could not protect you. Maybe having read of our loss out of love had left you to us.

There was a short note left; John brought the note to Rose. It read, "I hope my little Rose-wing will be free to fly, my shadow will cover the moon." We thought she was telling us that she would be watching over you.

Lisa went and got the brown paper bag. Taking out the little dainty slippers and the crimson velvet dress painstakingly stitched, both Lisa and Rose looked at the love that had gone into this delicate work, started to cry. Soon John had his arms around the both of them, let them have their cry. Then he joined them.

Lisa was handing the paper bag with the items and note inside to Rose saying, "They are yours now. Keep them close, some day they will tell you where you came from."

Rose was a popular girl in school, oft times getting her picture in the paper; some times as a cheerleader, a winner in an essay contest or being on the debate team.

The night she graduated from high school with honors was a proud moment for her parents. Walking up to get her diploma they thought she was stunning and so mature. That night there was a party at their house for a few of her friends.

In the next week she would be enrolled in a nurses program at U of M at the Duluth campus. Always wanting to help someone, perhaps working as a traveling nurse for one of the welfare offices would be a possibility. This way she would be able to get out to the poor, perhaps the reservation. She had talked this over with her parents, they agreed. They had saved so their daughter could go to college.

The last couple years Rose had struck up a relationship with Tony the barber. Tony had his little shop downtown was somewhat older and liked to say he was a half-breed, always talking about his Indian heritage. Rose always felt safe there, the stories she enjoyed, always feeling a little prettier when she left his shop. When Tony found she was leaving for college, he told her this hair cut was on the teepee! Laughing, she assured him she would be back.

Lisa had a hard time letting Rose go. They had driven to Duluth, the apartment was small but they loved it. Rose said they would get tired of her coming home; Lisa and John had a few tears on their way home. Knowing this was going to be a huge turning point in their life.

Like high school had flown by, college was the same. Rose was like a sponge, never taking the summer off, in college full time, getting a degree in nursing, studying some law and business courses. It was in June that she drove to her parents. You would think it had been a lifetime, understanding, Lisa feeling the same way. Having called, Lisa had her favorite meal, chicken and dumplings and fresh caramel rolls with cold milk.

Sitting around, talking into the evening, getting up early going to church, running into some friends she hadn't seen in years. One boy, Donald, she hardly recognized. He seemed very interested in her.

At 1:00 the next afternoon she hit the barbershop, Tony was elated! He wanted to know all about her, what she was going to do. Noticing he was aging a little more, gray at the temples, throwing him for a loop when she asked him outright, "Tony, why haven't you made an honest man of yourself and gotten married?" He said, "The right squaw never came along?" He didn't split a gut but he could have.

Then saying, "Girl, what are you going to be doing? I have heard that Cass County is looking for a traveling nurse, two days a week people would come to her office, three days a week traveling the county, checking on people. I would guess a bunch of down and out Indian kids and their mothers."

Rose thought, Tony, you just hit the nail on the head with that last statement.

Early the next morning driving to Walker in Cass County, she had no trouble finding the offices. At first no one knew about the openings. Then, she was talking to a supervisor who said they were just starting to put it together, saying what the job would be.

Rose had information with her showing all of her degrees, stating, this is what she had trained for, stating she was half Indian.

When she left, she was to start the next week. The first week would be setting up the offices. The pay at first would not be the best but doing what one wanted most would have its rewards.

The first two weeks were hectic, Mothers coming in with their young children just by the word of mouth. My God, how many sick and poor are there, oft times staying late to see them? Some mothers were very clean as was their children, some not having decent shoes or clothes. Many of the children had white fathers that never showed up, just the mothers.

On her traveling days she might be at Federal Dam, Ballclub or Deer River, never surprised any more what she would see or hear, as lots of the mothers would unburden their woes. She was learning that incest was a common thing here. Many of the girls and squaws were not married to the men they were living with. The main food in some shacks was beer. Many of the back yards were dumps with a couple of broken down cars sitting among the trees. No electricity had yet reached some of the areas and most of the roads were nearly impassible.

It is so easy to judge when you are not this poor? How do you come out of these shacks, lean-to's with outhouses out back and in many cases, no running water. Seeing this, you would almost think you were in another country. Then you would drive up to a place, beautifully cared for with good friendly people. Although many of them were down and out, they were a proud Indian nation.

Many of the Indians lived a meager existence; hunting, ricing, some had small farms and there were the trappers. There were some that had small businesses and many held jobs in the woods. There were never enough well paying jobs. Many collected from the welfare system or the reservations federal programs.

Rose, driving home from work was thinking there are whites that lived in squalor, some of them showing no signs of wanting to work, who worked the system. Many were heavy drinkers.

What could she do to help her people; there was only one of her. Thinking of a saying, "You must take a first step to get where you are going." She had taken two steps.

As she drove there was a half moon with some darker clouds drifting over it, what could that mean? The note left at her parents was always with her.

Rose had been working seven months now, thinking there was nothing more to be seen from the passing of a child or a mother. Lots of the time with no father present. What is to be done with these children?

Getting an early start on a cold winter morning she was driving to the Dick Alger's place on Hwy 46 on the reservation some 35 miles. They had several children reported sick. Getting into her car looking to the east, hanging in the sky was a blood red moon with dark clouds partly hiding it. Was this an omen, something bad was about to happen? As she was driving she couldn't help feeling uneasy. Arriving at the Alger's place soon after sunup, Dick the father met her at the door, the mother and children still in bed. Alger's was happy to see her, treating her with the utmost respect. Soon she was seeing each child, one at a time, making notes on each after examining them. The mother was the last and couldn't thank her enough for coming so far on a cold day. Rose could see the house was old and run down, the inside clean and neat.

The family had terrible colds, runny noses. Giving the mother instructions making sure they would be getting the proper food and water. She had some cold medicine that was to be given as per instructions.

This had taken the morning. As she was leaving, Alger's stopped her at the door. Quietly saying, "This may not be any of my business; there is a house about five miles down the road on your way back. It has different colored shingles on the buildings. There is a small woman there who is a seamstress. She was to drop off a few items here a week ago, this has never happened before, when she said she would be here, she would be. Could you stop by to see if she's alright. The lady's name is Susan Whitebird?" Getting a few more instructions, Rose said she would.

Rose was intently looking for the small house. Finally, that had to be the place. There were no tracks leading in, no smoke from the chimney. It looked deserted. It appeared everything needed repairing; an old car sitting off by itself with snow on it, the outhouse in back with no tracks to it, the windmill for water, a small garage with a sagging roof like most places out here and no electricity.

Nothing to indicate someone had been here. Standing for some time, turning to walk away, stopping she tried the door, it swung open. The stove was cold, the water bucket frozen solid, going to the pantry, frozen potatoes on the counter. The place was tidy, no wood inside the house, a little white peddle sewing machine in the corner. I'm wasting my time. It had two small bedrooms and an enclosed porch. The one bed room had a bed without covers on it. Looking into the other bedroom, it could be seen, the covers were piled high. No one could be seen. Turning to leave, almost to the front door, stopping, had she seen something, a few strands of dark hair up over a pillow? No, no one had been here for some time.

A chill ran up her spine, turning, walking to the bedroom door, looking, there were a few strands! She knew what she would find. Quietly walking to the head of the bed, a few strands of dark hair protruded from under the blankets. Pausing for a moment, reaching, lifting the blankets slowly, there appeared a small, middle aged

Indian woman. Reaching over, touching, she was cold. Almost putting the covers down, was there a movement? Had she taken a breath? At first feeling the side of the throat, nothing, holding there steady, there was a slight pulse. What to do, there weren't any phones?

Rose had never been in this situation. Having the strange feeling she knew the person laying there. Getting her thermometer, taking her temperature, it was down to 94. Thinking back to the medical books, she knew this was probably a severe hypothermia case. The standard thing to do was to call an ambulance, get them to a hospital but this was not an option. Putting the blanket back over her head, she went out into the cold, bringing in a couple armloads of wood, opening the barrel stove door, tearing up some old newspaper, there was a small wooden box that she broke up, putting it on the paper in the stove, then carefully laying some of the firewood into the stove at angles so the flames from below would catch them on fire. In only a few minutes there was a hardy flame. It would take the cold out of the room. Going back, she brought in the rest of the wood, then to her car to retrieve a thermos of hot chocolate she always carried with her, just in case.

Looking at her watch, it was 11:30 am; knowing what had to done. This was going to be the hardest part knowing a person with hyperthermia can be warmed up too quickly, it must be slow.

Standing by the heating barrel stove, she took off her shoes, leaving her socks on, stripping down to her panties, taking off her bra, leaving them all on a chair to stay warm. She walked the cold floor into the bedroom. Lifting the covers, she saw the woman a thin nightgown. Then she was in bed trying to snuggle in close to the small frail lady, knowing that the person's body heat could be the best way to transfer heat to the other person in a slow manner. Heating a hypothermic person too quickly can cause a heart attack and kill them. She was starting to chill knowing this was her only chance to save her. Putting her in the car, she wouldn't make it to the hospital. It wasn't long; she was starting to shiver, moving her body around, trying to stay close, wrapping her legs around and some times over. After a time, feeling body heat was starting to warm the covers. Shortly, climbing out of the bed, going to the stove, getting close, trying to warm herself. Jumping up and down trying to get her circulation going, thinking if someone walked in that door, they were in for a surprise!

Getting as warm as she could, taking the thermometer with her getting back into bed, reaching, taking her temperature, it was 95.5. It was more comfortable now at 1:00 p.m.

Lying there thinking, I know that face, where have I seen her before? It wasn't recently yet she had a feeling it was. The room itself was starting to warm. The hot barrel stove's heat was starting to creep into the bedroom. Soon she was up taken the frozen pail of water, putting it on the top of the barrel stove. It would take time; she may need warm water, not knowing if she would be able to get Susan Whitebird awake. If she could get her to swallow, one of the recommended treatments was to get warm liquids down a person so the core temperature would rise faster than their extremities.

Knowing the warm hot chocolate in the thermos had nourishment as well as liquid, would it be enough? She had backup on the stove. Lying there getting comfortable, she drifted off to sleep thinking if Susan woke up and was alert she would be wondering who this white woman was in bed with her. Awaking with a start, had Susan moved? She seemed to be breathing much deeper, feeling her pulse, it was much stronger. Taking the thermometer, she inserted it inside Susan's mouth and was about to pull it out when Susan reached, pulling it out! Her hand dropping back to the bed. Her temperature was almost 97. Rose was looking at the ceiling saying, "Thank you, God!" This is showing signs of working. Checking her watch, it was getting onto 4:00pm. Nothing more, no movement. Moving down further trying to get her legs in a more comfortable position, looking up she was staring into the blackest, most piercing eyes she had ever seen. Rose didn't know what to say; those eyes seemed to cut right through her. There was a weak smile. A small hand crept into hers and she was asleep. Rose didn't know quite what to do next. What she had been doing was working, a little more time. A half hour passed, she felt the little hand squeezing her finger. Looking, those eyes were open.

Rose said, "I don't know if you can understand me. I'm a traveling nurse from Cass County. I found you in a bad way and have been trying to help you, do you understand?"

A slight nod of the head, Susan seemed to be out of it somewhat.

Then, Rose was saying, "We have to see if we can get some warm liquid down you if we can to get you strong. You must go to the hospital as soon as I can move you. I'm going to get up now, get a few things done quickly. I won't leave you. Where had she seen that face?" Rose getting up, was soon dressed and getting into her warm cloths, going out, starting the car, turning the heater up, leaving it to warm up. She had most of a tank of gas. Coming back, putting more wood in the stove. It was getting toasty warm. Taking the thermos, going to the bedroom, her eyes were more alert. Sitting on the bed, she said, "My name is Rose-wing Paradise, can you tell me yours, do you understand me?"

A flicker of recognition, then a whisper, "Susan Whitebird."

Rose replied, "It's important, I'm a nurse, we must handle you a certain way, if we can get you to sit up and cough for me, making sure you can swallow. We have to get some warm liquid down. We must warm you inside as much as we can. If the rest of your body warms too fast, you could have a heart attack. Let's try to prop you up with pillows."

Helping Susan to sit, packing the pillows behind her, Rose said, "Try coughing now."

She was weak. When had she last eaten or had water? Rose asked, "Do you think you could try to swallow something now?"

She nodded, yes.

Removing the top of the thermos, pouring just a couple of table-spoons of cocoa into it, holding her head, tipping the cup so she could drink, she thought that went well. Pouring more into the cup, taking their time, this went on for a half hour. Finally Susan shook her head, half the thermos was gone, she could take no more.

Rose said, "We'll try more later."

Looking, judging she could see she must have been sick for some time. A small woman down perhaps 25 to 30 pounds. The poor thing had been wasting away.

More of the warm cocoa, then she must get her dressed, keeping her warm so she could be driven to the hospital. She would look through the room for some socks and heavy clothing, some long socks if they could be found.

Rose had seen a chest in the other bedroom. Opening the top drawer, she found some heavy sweaters, they would do. Not looking for under things at this time, they would just get in the way. Opening the bottom drawer there was a brown paper bag, putting it on top of the dresser, pulling some long socks from the drawer. Turning to leave, maybe there was something in the bag. Taking it to the bed, she turned it on its side, emptying some things on the bed.

It was almost like her mind quit working, she couldn't move or breathe. She stood there staring, feeling weak; she knew what she was seeing. Remembering the brown bag she had at home, on the bed in golden velvet a pair of slippers with the finest of hand stitching. Next to the slippers, a golden dress, a different color than her crimson colored dress but complete replicas. She knew where she had seen that face, going to the small mirror on the wall, looking, it was unmistakable.

This was her mother, what had she gone through for me? I have to be as strong as she is, then grabbing a towel, she couldn't hold it. Putting it over her face, the racking sobs were coming. All these years, it was coming out.

Looking in the mirror, Rose thought, "This has to stop; I have to get her to the hospital."

It wasn't easy cleaning up, she mustn't see this. "I will talk to her when the time is right," Rose told herself.

Getting the clothes together she would be putting on her, the slippers and dress into the bag, running them out to the car. Then she was helping Susan dress. Taking the pillows and blankets out to the car, how would she get her to the car? She left the front door ajar.

Sitting down, Susan finished the last of the warm chocolate. Sure now she was well bundled, she reached over picking up her mother like a doll, carrying her to the car. As Rose was carrying her, a funny thought ran through her mind, not remembering where she had heard it, "He's not heavy, he's my brother."

Rose knew this was the last time Susan Whitebird would live here. Going back to close the door, looking at the little white sewing machine, she would be back for it.

With Susan in the back seat, Rose was in hurry but not taking any chances on this road and certainly not with the treasure she had in the back. As she drove, oft times she was looking in the rear view mirror at the sleeping woman in the back.

Rose drove to the back of the hospital in Grand Rapids. This was the closest with some very good doctors. She was ringing the bell when an orderly came to the door, one she recognized, she had been here before. He didn't wait for a wheel chair, simply picking her up and carrying her to the emergency room laying her on a bed. It was early evening; a doctor and two nursed were tending to Susan. Rose explained how she had found the woman and the condition she was in. How she had slowly warmed her and the warm liquid she had given her. The staff took over.

While at the office doing the paperwork, Rose told the secretaries she would be responsible for all cost.

The doctor came to Rose saying Susan is a sick woman; she isn't out of the woods and wouldn't have made it another day. They would be working with her the rest of the night in the ICU.

"You probably saved her life; it couldn't have been handled better. Get some sleep, you'll need it tomorrow."

Rose was tired but still had something she had to do. Driving to her parents, she would be staying there tonight. She had a little place of her own by the lake but tonight she had to talk to John and Lisa, her parents on what she had discovered in the paper bag. While putting them back, she had discovered not only the slippers and dress but some newspaper clippings. One had her picture on it but she hadn't had the time to look further.

Pulling into the driveway, the lights were on. Good, they were still up. Out of her car so excited, she could hardly contain herself. Rushing in, "Mom, Dad", they were thinking something must be wrong. Coming to her saying, "Honey, what is it?"

Rose lifted the brown bag, Lisa seemed to know, John stood like, "What's going on?"

Then she said, "Sit at the table, I have something to show you."

When they were seated she came to them reaching into the bag bringing out a golden satin dress, reaching in, and then the little slippers were sitting by the dress. Digging into the bag, a handful of newspaper clippings were spread on the table. Some of them very old, one newer one stood out, a picture of Rose accepting her college diploma, another from the Cass Lake News mentioning the recent hiring of a traveling nurse, a Rose-Wing Paradise.

John sat there stupefied, Lisa's mouth was working, but no words coming out. Then Lisa asked, "Where, how did you find all of this? This may help you find..."

Rose ,standing there with her hand over her heart, the other palm out reaching to them, tears rolling down her cheeks, looking at the newspaper clippings on the table she realized there had been a moment at the old cabin she thought there had been a flicker of recognition in the eyes of Susan Whitebird. Susan Whitebird knew who she was all the time, yet said nothing, still asking for nothing, still trying to protect her. It took some time to pull herself together. Sitting at the table; holding her parents hands, telling them fully about the moon that morning, where she had been, someone asking her to look in on a lady that may be in trouble. At first not thinking anyone was there. Something had pushed her on, she had done her best. Now Susan Whitebird, her mother was in the hospital, maybe being put in a coma. She may not make it. She would be there early in the morning. It may be days, she was a very sick woman. Any change and the doctor was to call.

They talked late, her parents praying for Susan, they were with Rose helping in any way they could. Saying that when she got well, there was an extra bedroom here, they could never repay the debt they owed Susan.

At 10:00 the next morning the doctor came in to tell Rose he had been there overnight but had gone home to get a couple hours of sleep and told her it was just a matter of time now by all accounts.

"It was amazing she had made it this far under the conditions you told me about," said the doctor. "I have a good feeling we will know soon."

Rose was spending her time between the hospital and her parents. They had gone through the newspaper clippings. How had Susan managed to get some of what she had? There was a picture of Rose in front of the parent's house about seven years old.

Three days later the doctor said they would know that day. It was near 1:00 when she noticed Susan stirring. Being a nurse, she knew it was going to take some time. A quarter to 4:00, looking up, those black eyes were half open, seemingly trying to focus on her. A little more time, Rose walked over, picking up the small hand squeezing it gently. The eyes came open. Susan was holding Rose's hand.

Rose said, "Mother, I know who you are, looking into those

eyes."

A couple of tears spilled down Susan's cheek. She was biting her lip, and then a wistful smile appeared. Something was happening to her, someone who truly loved her. She could feel the love remembering the naked body in bed saving her life; her daughter.

Susan knew there were going to be difficult times never having anyone close. Rose had been her love from the minute she was born. Always secluded, no one to talk to, could she make those adjustments? She would be in the hospital at least a week, Rose almost never left her side, always talking to her trying to draw her out. She was so tired. On the third day they had her sitting up in bed feeding her intravenously. A few pounds were going back on. The strength was returning. On the fifth day Susan had a surprise, Lisa and John came up to meet her. Leaving Rose with them had been the right choice.

Susan found as a woman talking to Lisa about their daughter came easily, a little more hesitant with John. Then as he talked about the room he was getting ready for her, she warmed to his affectionate smile.

Rose would work to arrange that Susan would be living with them until she was strong enough to move to Rose's house. Rose would be staying with them also.

Susan was laying there trying to put this all together from the little cabin to moving in with her daughter. How had this all happened and so fast?

She knew when the time was right, Rose would be after her for the story on how she had been left with John and Lisa. Could she ever tell Rose the entire truth?

Her past was almost like a fog, the years, how much could she remember? Some parts stood out in contrast, never to be forgotten.

She could vaguely remember waking up as a child, lying on a blanket on the chilly porch which was to be her room for some years. How had she come to live with the Nelson's was never revealed to her. They were white as was their son, Del. She was Indian and they never let her forget it. When very young, they taught her to do chores. If they were not done properly, the razor strap on her legs a couple times were a sure reminder.

She was oft times referred to as lazy. Their son was their joy. As he aged, was allowed to come and go, never required to do much and if he did would always complain. Susan had balked a few times but soon learned better. A few times she was allowed to ride to Cass Lake in their old car.

Although small, Susan was strong. As she was aging, she was required to keep the wood box full. She and Del got along fairly well the first few years, him, being five or six years older. She could often remember the most fun she had. It was in the cold of winter, the river was frozen over. They would slide down the high hill in back on the big toboggan, Del screaming and then laughing coming off the high hill. They would shoot almost across the river.

Warren, the father had a small garden, Susan was his helper there, at times he treated her quite well telling her what a great job she had done. She loved the praise. Then he had his drinking days, stay out of striking distance. Also, Faye, the mother seemed jealous of any praise Susan might get. She would not realize until many years later, reveling in the little praise she received, she was regarded as their little slave, to do their bidding.

The mother was a part time seamstress doing small jobs for pay. Noticing Susan watching her intently as she sewed with a little pedal sewing machine when Susan was almost seven, Faye walked in unexpectedly; Susan was sitting at the machine sewing a little dress together. Faye walked over slapping Susan saying, "Haven't I told you never to touch this machine?" Susan ran to the porch.

Faye started to walk away then looked down at the little dress Susan had been sewing together. Not believing what she was seeing, she was a seamstress and couldn't do that quality of work.

Faye called Susan to her, asking her how long she had been using the machine. Susan replies, "At least a couple of weeks." That week she started to bring more things home to be repaired. Teaching Susan to sew from patterns, there was no play time in the house. Susan was spending much of the time on the machine. Faye was happy, never sharing the money she received.

Susan thought she was about nine years old when Del started hanging around her more, making funny remarks. Some times he would try to wrestle with her, putting his hands where he shouldn't. One time he tried sliding his hands into her jeans, she slapped him across the face. He left mad, he left her alone for some time.

About a year later, Faye and Warren were going to be gone all day; Del came in from the outside and was standing by the door. Looking up from her sewing she noticed he had grown so much the last year. He came over, standing behind her starting to give her a back rub. She told him to stop, instead he slid his arms around her picking her up while she struggled, carrying her onto the porch and onto her blanket, forcing her onto the floor pinning her with his weight.

She tried to move, and then he was saying, "Do you like this?" Crying, she told him to stop, "I'm going to tell your mother."

He said, "Go ahead, she won't believe you."

Finally he let her go, going into his bedroom and shutting his door. Shortly, he came out seeming more relaxed and left for the outdoors.

Later Warren and Faye drove in from town bringing in a few things, then Warren was outside to do some chores.

Susan walked up to Faye starting to tell her what Del had done to her. She found herself on the floor. She hadn't seen it coming. Faye was saying, "You ungrateful tramp after all we've done for you accusing my son of such a thing!"

That was just the start of it. What could she do? There was nowhere to run. Every time they went to town, he was after her. It wasn't a month later, he raped her, she was crying. How could she fight him off? There seemed to be nothing she could do. One time Faye asked her how she was getting the bruises on her arms. She started to say something, then she remembered the last time. When they were gone, Del would tell her she was his to do with as he pleased. A couple of times when she wouldn't do what he was wanting he got his father's razor strap out, he knew how to use it on her bare bottom.

When the parents were there, everything seemed normal. He told her if she ever mentioned what he had been doing the last few years he would use a knife on her. She believed him; he was without any sense of mercy.

She was getting close to 15 years old when Warren took sick; the doctors gave him three months. He was gone in two. Del was now the head of the house and would be gone drinking almost every day coming in late at night. He no longer cared what his mother might think, taking Susan by the arm pulling her into the bedroom.

Three months after Warren died; Faye had a heart attack in the morning and was gone by noon. There was a burial, three people were there, the minister was one of them. From then on Del made sure Rose was his personal servant. He had her taking in things to be repaired. It was not hard to get work as she had acquired a reputation as the finest in the area.

Warren and Faye had been gone a year. Del had been gone a few hours. Thinking this may be her only chance, she took off up over the hill by the river. Following the river, she was crossing the road, there he sat waiting. Throwing her in the truck, he took her home. Taking her in the bedroom, he raped her. Getting up smiling he proceeded to beat the hell out of her. Even though he threatened her the next day, she couldn't get up. It was a few days before she was moving.

Two months later, she suspected she was carrying. It was some time before he knew. Not happy, he said, "We don't need any crying kids around here." Del said to her, he had heard you could get rid of it with a clothes hanger. For some reason he didn't try but he was making her life hell.

The day of Rose's birth, Susan was alone and didn't know how she made it through the day.

Having turned off the gas lamp so it was dark when Del stumbled into the house that night, not coming to bother her. She had the baby bundled in some blankets. The next morning when Del got up, looking at her, he knew and was mad as hell threatening to take the kid and throw her in the river, acting surly the rest of the day. It had snowed during the night. The river was half frozen over.

Susan was having a rough time; the baby was colicky, crying a lot. She had torn giving birth; Del was after her and wouldn't wait much longer. Threatening her and blaming the child, she knew he was capable of killing the child. He was still bringing work home for her to do on the machine.

The last couple months had brought some relief to Susan; he was drinking so much he couldn't perform, blaming the baby. One night in a rage he left the bed running, picking her up by one arm, threatening to slam her to the floor. Susan, in a panic had followed, getting on her knees, pleading, crying, "Put the baby down, I will help you."

This seemed to be the power he wanted. Turning, he didn't put her down; he threw her some eight feet. She bounced off the bed onto the floor. She lay there screaming, Susan trying to go to her almost had her arm yanked off. As she was dragged back into the bedroom, a half hour later, Del was passed out.

Susan came quietly out of the bedroom to her crying baby. She knew the rages Del was throwing; the baby would be dead in a few days. She couldn't live with the violence and spankings she was receiving. She could only hold him back so long.

At about 2:00 p.m., Del left heading for the bar, most often getting home between midnight and 1:00 a.m. Susan knew she was going to do something, she had to. It had to be when he was most vulnerable. Taking a skinning knife, she put it under the mattress. The baby, unable to sleep, hurting from her injuries.

Turning out the gas lights, the house was fully dark. There was a brilliant full moon almost like day outside. She lay cradling Rose to her, listening, never daring to go to sleep lest he come for the baby.

At 12:30 a.m., hearing the car drive in, waiting, not coming in. Wondering she crept to the door. He was lying in the driveway passed out in the cold snow. Looking to the tool shed, there was the toboggan leaning against the wall. Looking to the full moon she had a thought. Dressing quickly, she was soon pulling the sled to Del on the snow. He was a large man; she finally had him on it. Getting some wire, she wired his feet to the front of the sled, then wiring his arms on both sides to the edges. Then she started to pull, not to the house but in the direction of the big hill where they used to slide down to the frozen river. It was some hundred yards away. She was a little woman, this took her some time. Del was starting to stir; it had taken her almost an hour. She now had the toboggan at the top of the hill.

Now he was fully awake struggling to get free, cursing at her. Lying as he was, he could look down the deep slope at the ice on the side of the river and the dark current as it flowed by.

Without hesitation, Susan gave the sled a push. It started to pick up speed; the screams did bring back memories of the past except she didn't hear the laughter. It was reaching the bottom, shooting over the river bank onto the ice and then onto the water where it settled, starting to sink. The screams echoing along the river bank.

Susan slowly walked back to the cabin. Rose was sleeping safe now. If anyone asked, she would tell them Del had come home insisting they go for a toboggan ride in the middle of the night, she had refused. Leaving by himself, she had never seen him or the sled again.

Lighting the gas lantern, she rummaged through the bottom drawer taking out a newspaper clipping that when she had first read it had intrigued her, the word paradise stood out. A place she always wanted for her daughter, Rose. Reading it, she thought it was an omen. Had God put it there for her to pick up? Having just deciding a new home for Rose had to be found.

Loving Rose so much, she must have a better life than I have lived. She was good at getting information; no one seemed to know she had been asking questions. Soon she had a plan, knowing where John and Lisa went to church and where they lived. Waiting for the right moment, they left for church. Watching from her hiding place, in a few minutes she was in with Rose fixing chairs so she couldn't get out, then driving her old Plymouth coup home, biting her lip all the way.

The years had gone fast. When she could, picking up a paper hoping something would be in them, always on the alert for some word. Through the years she had been able to get a few pictures.

Much of her time trying to make a living, attending her little garden, the little frozen potatoes in the kitchen at her cabin had been the last of her food. The little white peddle sewing machine had at last broken down. She had been sick for some time, at last slipping under the covers. Looking through the windows at the blood red moon, she would soon be with Mother Earth.

Slowly waking from her dream, there was rose beaming holding her hand.

Susan, the first day home with her daughter, thought she had never lived in such elegance; a refrigerator with no ice or sawdust, a toilet in the house you could turn a handle and get running water, turn a dial and cook food, such food in the cupboards they could be made in minutes and a box on the table you could sometime see a person on it, then they would be gone in the snow. There were lots of paths just outside the door, sometimes she would walk in the solitude of the evening. Gaining weight, her strength had almost returned, never thinking she could enjoy someone around her so much!

She had been helping Rose clean and paint the bedroom that was to be hers in the little house by the lake.

The day had come, it was with regret. She and Lisa had become very close; she loved John who knew much of her story yet treated her with respect.

Susan had been out of the hospital a couple months, she and Rose had talked at great length. Having told everything she could remember over the last years. The beatings, how she had been forced, thinking Del would come home one night and harm Rose, the knife hidden under the mattress, instead he came home insisting they go sledding on the toboggan, he was drunk. Refusing, he had left by himself; he and the sled were never seen again.

She had struggled a few years until rescued by her daughter. Susan was now working for a Penney's store as a sales clerk and a seamstress. The manager said he was amazed at how fast she caught on.

Rose and Susan had been going to church with her parents each Sunday. At one time in church Rose had met a boy named Donald, with whom she had gone to school with, hardly recognizing him. Now finding he was a doctor of dentistry, many of the children she was working with were in need.

Spending much time discussing the needs of the children, they had dinner together. He had now been invited to Sunday dinner of chicken and dumplings with caramel rolls at the Paradise's.

Rose was still working many hours as a traveling nurse had been amazed at how fast her mother's recovery had been. She had a job and was well respected. Coming home to her one evening there was a car parked across the street.

Walking into the entry she heard the most beautiful voice like a Meadow Lark singing across the fields to its mate while flying high and free. Sitting at the table was Tony the barber mesmerized; I walked out the door to a beautiful moon.

~

These stories might make
us ask ourselves,
"Can murder be justified?"